THE RESPECTABLE MURDERERS

THE RESPECTABLE
MURDERERS

Social Evil and Christian Conscience

Paul Hanly Furfey

HERDER AND HERDER

1966
HERDER AND HERDER NEW YORK
232 Madison Avenue, New York 10016

Nihil obstat: Thomas J. Harte, C.Ss.R., Ph.D.
                 Censor Deputatus
Imprimatur: + Patrick A. O'Boyle
                 Archbishop of Washington
                 December 7, 1965

Library of Congress Catalog Card Number: 66–26816
© 1966 by Herder and Herder, Inc.
Manufactured in the United States

Therefore God sends upon them a strong delusion that they may believe falsehood, that all may be judged who did not believe the truth, but took delight in wickedness.

2 THESS. 2, 11–12

PREFACE

Social criticism is less likely to be based on abstract principles of right and wrong than on the standards which happen to prevail in the critic's own social class. This is unfortunate, but understandable. In the give-and-take of daily life one constantly meets approval and disapproval which are prescribed by the standards of one's associates. The acceptance of these standards becomes so automatic that they gradually are accepted as the ethics of the group. Even when large social issues are judged, these same standards are likely to be used. Thus social criticism can easily be biased by class consciousness.

The most widely respected social criticism is likely to be that which emanates from the middle and upper social classes. Here belong the newspaper editors, the radio and television commentators, the spokesmen for business interests, and others who make it their profession to comment on social issues. Members of the lower class are obviously less well equipped to formulate their opinions and they have less access to the media of communication to express them. The result is a class bias which passes lightly over the flaws and deficiencies of the higher classes and discusses with great emphasis the sins of, for example, slum dwellers.

The present book will examine certain outstanding examples of the social evils which have been condoned by the decent and respectable citizens of the time. I have deliberately chosen examples whose immorality is beyond dispute. Certainly, no one will question the heinous moral evil of the slaughter of the European Jews, of the Atlantic slave trade, or of American Negro slavery. After reading the strong language of the Second Vatican Council, surely no Catholic can presume to defend the massacre of civilian noncombatants in the Second World War. The injustice of extreme poverty existing in our country's present era of unparalleled prosperity must also be evident, although in this case it is less easy to place the blame exactly.

In discussing these social evils, I have tried to present the facts with all possible scientific objectivity. If the reader finds the book somewhat low-keyed emotionally, let him realize that this is intentional. Nothing could be more eloquent than the stark realities. No language can add to the horror of the simple truth that under the Third Reich more than five million Jews were put to death in cold blood.

There is a particularly potent reason why the Christian thinker should force himself to face social issues without the bias which comes from accepting uncritically the viewpoint of the upper and middle classes. This is the example of Christ Himself. The persons He denounced, the rich and the powerful, the scribes and the Pharisees, were eminently respectable members of the favored classes. The only persons, as far as we know, against whom He used physical violence were the merchants trafficking in the Temple precincts. He earned the hatred of the respectable, and it was they who compassed His death. Certainly, they are not true followers of Christ who do not repudiate all bias in favor of those who were His enemies.

But it is hard to repudiate the respectable. A strong delusion

12

operates in their favor. The very fact that their viewpoint is defined as respectable makes it difficult to discard. This, however, is the task of the Christian, as it is also the task of the present book.

Paul Hanly Furfey
March 20, 1966

CONTENTS

1

The Respectable Murderers

It is an infinitely tragic fact that the greatest crimes of history are committed with the cooperation or at least with the passive consent of the solid citizens who constitute the stable backbone of the community. The sporadic crimes that soil the front pages, the daily robberies, assaults, rapes, and murders are the work of individuals and small gangs. They are committed by manifest criminals whom the community despises and punishes. But the great evils, the persecutions, the unjust wars of conquest, the mass slaughters of the innocent, the exploitations of whole social classes—these crimes are committed by the organized community under the leadership of respectable citizens.

When the guilt of the "respectable" is discussed, it is evident that the term is being applied in a somewhat special sense which it is necessary to define before going further. The "respectable," as the word is used here, includes first of all the community's power structure, governors, senators, judges, generals, corporation presidents, large investors; it includes, secondly, the molders of public opinion such as prominent clergymen, editors, professors, and experts of various sorts whose views are "respected." But "respectable" is used here to mean as well the followers of such persons. There exists a whole class of lesser people who from afar ape the manners of the great and assent to their decisions. All these people, the prominent and the obscure, set the tone of the community. They are the respectable and what they do is the respectable thing to do. Their viewpoint is expressed in community action.

As a random example of the crimes of the respectable, one may think of religious persecution. Under the Roman Empire the nascent Christian Church was certainly no threat to public order; yet it was persecuted savagely. Among those who followed this policy of persecution there were humane emperors like Trajan. There was even a philosopher of some standing, Marcus Aurelius. Occasionally, some of these high-minded rulers had passing scruples; but the cruel persecutions went on.[1] There were indeed brutal and degraded persecutors like Nero; yet, whoever was emperor, the actual process of persecution made use of that admirable system of law and law enforcement which perhaps constituted Rome's greatest contribution to Western civilization. The Christian martyrs were not murdered by criminals living beyond the pale of the law. Generally speaking, they were executed after a trial in which the legal forms were observed. Respectable citizens approved.

Even within Christianity itself the same dismal story of persecution has been repeated. One may think of the Spanish Inquisition or of the sufferings of Catholics during the penal days in England. It is indeed true that some of this intra-Christian savagery can be ascribed to politics rather than to religion. Also some of it was unplanned and was due, for example, to sudden outbreaks of mob fury. However, due allowance having been made for such exceptions, the grim reality is that a great many

18

cruel deaths were the result of deliberate policy called for by religious leaders and approved by the upright, the pious, and the God-fearing. Persecutions were not the illegal actions of criminals; they were the legally sanctioned work of the respectable.

It is hard to understand how a person could seriously profess the Christian religion of love and yet turn with such brutal fury on his fellow Christians. Indeed, it is hard to understand *any* of the crimes of the respectable. The word "respectability" itself implies an acceptance of moral principle, a willingness to be guided by reason, and a self-control which can rise above passion. The respectable person seems to be the very antithesis of the criminal. Why, then, are the eminently respectable responsible for so many of the great crimes of history?

In order to see the problem in its proper light, it is important to bear in mind that a man may be guided in his decisions either by a consciously understood, ethico-religious code of conduct or by the customs prevalent in his community.

Thoughtful men at all times and places have recognized that certain acts are good and certain acts are bad—and this by the very nature of these acts. Thus it is generally agreed that exercising justice, mercy, bravery, and fidelity are good and that committing robbery, murder, treachery, and rape are bad. In spite of many disagreements, there is yet a certain solid consensus among the world's ethical systems—a fact which can be reasonably explained by the existence of what may be broadly termed natural law.[2] Religion adds the weight of its authority to this consensus, strengthens it by teaching the existence of divine sanctions, and

19

prescribes further duties relating to social worship. In the decisions of his daily life, a man who applies the ethico-religious principles which he accepts is guided by what we call conscience.

But conscience, as ordinary experience attests, is not the only possible principle of action. It is equally possible to follow uncritically the example of others, to accept prevailing customs without questioning their rightness or wrongness. Every community has its prescribed way of acting in specified situations—what sociologists call mores.[3] Those who violate such mores are punished in various formal or informal ways. For example, the mores of a community usually prescribe courtesy, diligence, and honesty, and the man who is habitually discourteous is punished by a degree of social ostracism, the conspicuously lazy worker is fired, the thief is sent to jail. Thus the pressure to conform is constant.

Conscience and the mores do not always and necessarily agree. This is understandable because the two have different bases. Conscience is founded on a personal response to abstract principles which are intended to apply at all times and places. In contrast, the mores are founded on nothing but custom; and custom is notoriously mutable. One need not be an anthropologist to realize how widely mores diverge from people to people and from age to age. What is considered sheer cruelty at one time and place may pass for manly firmness elsewhere. What one society calls thrift another may consider miserliness. Dueling may be either murder or the supreme mark of a gentleman of honor according to the prevailing mores.

The mores of a society may or may not be in agreement with sound ethico-religious principles. One may define as moral that society in which close agreement exists, and as paramoral that society in which the agreement is notably poor. It is necessary to coin a new term and call the latter type of society "paramoral" rather than "immoral" because the latter term would imply total corruption; and a totally corrupt society could hardly survive at all. What is here meant by a paramoral society is one in which at least a few conspicuous mores are clearly immoral. In such societies the "respectable" thing to do may be a clear violation of the objective moral law; so that those who persecute religion or exploit defenseless minorities are honored and elected to public office. Thus by a strange perversion crime becomes a badge of decency. A paramoral society is therefore an ethically sick society, one in which custom encourages evil in at least some aspects of community life.

The conscientious citizen living in a paramoral society suffers from a stress which can be simply overwhelming. If he follows his conscience he will perhaps suffer social ostracism, perhaps financial ruin, or even martyrdom. But if he yields to the social pressure he may pervert the essential purpose of his existence, for it *is* possible to decide frankly to follow the mores in defiance of conscience. To do this, and candidly accept the guilt, is not easy. Thus it must have required a certain courage to write as Patrick Henry did in a letter to a friend: "Would any one believe that I am Master of Slaves of my own purchase! . . . However culpable my Conduct, I will so far pay my devoir to Virtue, as to own the excellence and rectitude of her Precepts and to lament my want of conformity to them."[4] There is hope for such a man.

Faced with the dichotomy between the mores of a paramoral society on the one hand and the dictates of his conscience on the other, cannot a man in some way evade the choice? Is there perhaps some way in which he can at the same time avoid the penalties for defying the mores and still avoid the agony of violating his deepest principles? It is evident that there are, indeed, many such ways. One may tacitly follow the mores and yet somehow stifle or deceive one's conscience and thus avoid feelings of guilt. This self-deception is not a happy solution. A refusal to face the facts is a sort of voluntary moral blindness, certainly a fearful price to pay.

Everyone who has studied human conduct, from writers on the spiritual life to psychoanalysts, knows something about man's vast powers of moral self-deception. Because such deception is so easy, spiritual writers stress the importance of self-knowledge and founders of religious communities build regular examinations of conscience into their rules. Psychiatrists and specialists in dynamic psychology systematically catalogue the various techniques of human self-deception as "mental mechanisms" or "parataxes."[5] Some of the more common of these merit consideration here.

The simplest way to avoid an unpleasant fact is simply to refuse to think about it—the mechanism of repression. Unless one is a sadist, it is unpleasant to think about other people's sufferings; it is depressing to meditate on the distress of the poor or the victims of persecutions; better far to put such things out of one's mind. One reason why the solution of social problems proceeds so slowly is that people in general simply refuse to advert to the existence of these problems and to contemplate them in all their naked horror.

Then there is rationalization, the process of obviating an uncomfortable fact by fallacious logic. Thus it is frequently argued that one has no obligation to help the poor because they are lazy, shiftless, and undeserving. Or one may maintain that the Negro should not be given the vote because the colored race is inferior, and one may bolster this rationalization by allegedly scientific studies.[6] In fact, social problems are so complex both in their causes and in their effects that even the sincere and honest expert finds it difficult to understand them. Anyone who is less than completely sincere can quickly lose himself in a maze of half truths, fallacious arguments, and invalid generalizations.

A man may acknowledge both the existence of problems and the theoretical duty to do something about them, and yet deny that there is anything he can do: he may then excuse himself on the ground of impossibility. This acceptance of failure without trying is the mechanism of defeat, which may take various forms. A man may brood pessimistically about the ills of society in a chronic mood of depression; or he may reject the real world with all its cruelty, and endeavor to find refuge in a sort of fantasy world of his own, a world of romance and glamour, remote from all realities. But in every case the duty of *personal* action is evaded.

Possibly the most irritating mechanism of all is sublimation. One stifles a feeling of guilt by developing some public virtue of a bizarre and superficial sort. Thus a person tries to convince himself—and others as well—that so conspicuously virtuous a person as he obviously is could not possibly be lacking in a social conscience. The ardent church member who parades his religiosity while being shockingly unkind in his interhuman relations has nearly become a stock in trade of novels and movies. Equally stereotyped is the "old-maid shock reaction" of the sexually de-

23

prived woman who conceals her gnawing eroticism by engaging in a headlong campaign against pornography. This is hypocrisy, albeit often an unconscious hypocrisy. Obviously, it would be grossly unjust to accuse good people indiscriminately of this mechanism, because sublimation is one thing and genuine virtue is quite another; the former is disclosed by its unnatural and eccentric qualities. The fact remains, however, that hypocrisy, posing as virtue, promotes self-deception, confuses issues, and thus slows effective social reform.

The mental mechanisms which we have just discussed are by no means the only ones with which one can stifle conscience and embrace the mores of a paramoral society. What has been said, however, is enough to illustrate the point that the choice between conscience and evil mores is a choice which can be evaded. It is the easy solution; and it does bring the temporary satisfaction of avoiding both a break with society and the pain of guilt. The satisfaction, however, is never complete and lasting, for inevitably new stresses take the place of the old ones. Blinding oneself is not the best way to avoid the sight of ugly surroundings.

The mental mechanisms which stifle the social conscience have been described in the foregoing paragraphs as reactions of the individual. This is a valid assessment: individuals *do* use these unconscious devices to avoid feelings of guilt. However, there is another dimension to the problem. Not only the individual, but a community as a whole, can be affected by such mechanisms. Very clear instances of this are furnished by such recent examples of totalitarianism as Stalin's Russia and Hitler's Germany. Great evils existed in these countries, but there was no freedom to discuss them (repression). A vast network of propaganda, covering the schools, the press, the radio, explained away the defects of the regime (rationalization). Terroristic methods demonstrated to the common citizen the futility of revolt (defeat). A constant, systematic glorification of the system's advantages, real or alleged, obscured its injustices and cruelties (sublimation). The point is that it is not so much the individual citizen who turns to these mental mechanisms to lull his conscience as it is the state which forces them upon him.

But we need not consider Russia or Germany for examples of the phenomenon. In the sullenly segregated states of the American South, Negro citizens are today undergoing cruelties, indignities, and injustices which shock the vast majority of the country's citizens; yet there are many decent and respectable citizens, say, of Mississippi or Alabama, who seem genuinely blind to all this. This is partly because of individual reluctance to face the facts. Yet there is something more. Self-deception is part of the local southern culture. It is a rare clergyman who would preach his Sunday sermon on racial injustice; it is a rare teacher who would discuss the subject frankly in his classroom; it is a rare editor who would face the subject on his editorial page. Realistic discussion of race relations is repressed. Moreover, the topic is rationalized. The old, unjust stereotypes of the Negro and his personality are not recent, private inventions; they are part of the local folklore. Terror and the threats of terror discourage innovation and spread the mechanism of defeat. Finally, a wholly unrealistic but romantic and attractive picture of ante-bellum planta-

25

tion life has become traditional. Thus the pleasant myth obscures the unpleasant reality. It is a case of mass sublimation.

It is particularly painful to find an organized religious group lending the weight of its prestige to immoral mores. Yet we know this to be a constant temptation. The customs of religious leaders have an aura of divine sanction; therefore, even when these customs are evil, they may escape public criticism. The mechanism is common enough, one fears, in all religions, and has been anatomized in the classic case of the scribes and Pharisees of whom Christ said: "You pay tithes on mint and anise and cummin, and have left undone the weightier matters of the Law, right judgment and mercy and faithfulness."[7] These men were commendably careful about the duty of paying taxes, so that they did not overlook even their unimportant garden herbs. Yet they neglected the social virtues, "right judgment" which gives to every man his due, "mercy" which goes beyond the strict demands of justice, and "faithfulness" to pacts and promises.[8] The scribes and Pharisees had an extremely distorted sense of values which Jesus expressed with devastating irony when He accused them of "straining out the gnat but swallowing the camel."[9]

In this distortion of the moral sense, the social virtues are most likely to suffer—right judgment and mercy and faithfulness— especially as they apply to persons outside one's immediate orbit. A man may be just in his business dealings, an excellent family man, and upright in his relations with friends and associates; yet he may cooperate without a qualm in outrageous policies of social injustice, in the waging of an unjust war, or in the exploitation of a whole social class. Incredible as it may seem, it appears to be rather easy to swallow the camel.

26

We have discussed the painful and portentous fact that otherwise decent citizens have again and again cooperated actively in the great crimes of history, or have at least passively consented to them. Martyrs are rare. The ordinary citizen is lost in the mass. Partly this is because he deceives himself; partly it is because organized society, the state, both deceives and coerces him. This is a truism of overwhelming social importance. Decency and respectability prevent individual crime. Decent and respectable citizens on their own initiative rarely rob and murder and rape. Yet decency and respectability do not effectively hinder the crimes of society. On the contrary, decent and respectable citizens eagerly participate in them.

The moral training given in the home, the citizenship training given in the school, the religious training given in the churches cooperate in the fabrication of decent and respectable citizens. Only a slight minority choose clearly criminal careers. The decent and respectable majority consists of citizens who work quietly at their jobs, pay their just debts, are faithful to their friends, qualify as good parents and spouses, and avoid entanglements with the law. Each has his personal faults, no doubt, and his occasional lapses. Yet, all in all, the training they receive is "successful"—as far, that is, as the conventional morality is concerned.

However, if this typically decent and respectable citizen finds himself immersed in the stresses of a paramoral society, then his ethical and religious training erodes. He is tyrannized by dictators or swayed by mob passions or deceived by wily propaganda. As a member of a group he participates in crimes from which as an individual he would recoil with horror. Something is tragically wrong with our educational system. It is important to know *what* is wrong. It is *desperately* important to know.

Before an answer to the question just raised is attempted, it will be necessary to examine four concrete instances of paramoral societies and of the crimes of these societies in which the decent and the "God-fearing" cooperated.

2

American Negro Slavery

BEFORE examining, in the next chapter, an appalling example of national moral bankruptcy, perhaps the worst of our century—the Nazi slaughter of the Jews—it is desirable that we look at a moral aberration of earlier centuries which transcended all national boundaries, and which, in fact, flourished most vigorously in that country which proudly boasted of being "conceived in liberty and dedicated to the proposition that all men are created equal."

To understand slavery in America, it is not enough to study the plantation system. The subject as a whole must be studied, and to do this one must include the Atlantic slave trade. Plantation slavery could not have existed without this trade; and conversely the slave trade could not have flourished for centuries unless the planters had been eager customers. The Christian gentleman who bought a slave in Virginia made profitable the atrocities of the Guinea Coast.

The beginnings of the modern Negro slave trade go back to the fifteenth century, but it was only in 1619 that the first slaves were purchased in the English continental colonies; in that year twenty Negroes were sold at Jamestown from a Dutch vessel. In the early part of the seventeenth century only a few Negroes were owned in Virginia and their status seems to have been more that of indentured servants than of slaves. The rise of the plantation economy changed all that. There was an international demand for tobacco, and the efficient production of this crop called for a large supply of relatively unskilled workers. Negro slaves seemed to the planters to be the ideal answer to the demand for labor of this sort. In the 1660's Virginia and Maryland began to lay the legal foundations for slavery. The plantation system grew and slavery grew with it, so that soon it was extended to the production of other staples, rice, indigo, sugar, cotton. Although the system spread to the northern colonies, yet because it did not fit into the economy—not because it was viewed as immoral—it gradually died out. In the South, slavery developed and expanded simply because it solved an economic problem.[1]

The slave trade grew with the demand for slaves, so that in the eighteenth century it was highly organized and flourishing. Slaves were shipped from Africa to the West Indies and then later to the continental colonies, or directly to the latter. The traders were either English, typically from Liverpool, or American, usually from New England. Slaves ships made a triangular journey, from the home port to Africa, from Africa to the West Indies or a port in the continental colonies of the South, and then from there back to the home port. Thus a New England ship might carry a cargo of rum to Africa, then a cargo of slaves to the West Indies, and finally a cargo of molasses to the home port, where the molasses was distilled into rum and the process was repeated. During the second leg of the triangular journey, known as the Middle Passage, slaves were the only cargo.

Slave populations in the colonies grew so rapidly in the eighteenth century that the demand for imported slaves slackened. Also, in the natural-rights atmosphere of the time, a few people began to develop moral scruples over slavery. After the Revolution all the states banned the slave trade and in 1808 it was prohibited by national legislation.[2] In the meantime, however, in 1793, the cotton gin had been invented. It now became feasible to raise cotton on a large scale. At the same time the development of the factory system made the large-scale production of cotton textiles also feasible. Cotton proved to be the ideal crop for the plantations so that the demand for slaves was suddenly enormous. The faint moral reservations that had been voiced were swept aside, and the slave trade was revived. Legislation against the trade was enforced only halfheartedly. Although in 1820 Congress made the slave trade equivalent to piracy, a capital offense, no one was executed for the crime until the Civil War. There were less than 700,000 slaves at the time of the 1790 census; in 1860 there were almost four million.[3] Of course, most of this growth was due to natural increase; but it is significant that natural increase had to be supplemented by smuggling to keep up with the demand.

The bulk of the American slave trade was with West Africa.[4] This territory was at the time almost entirely under the control of native potentates, many of whom were extremely powerful. In the early days of the trade some captains, like the Englishman

31

John Hawkins, would raid the coast and enslave whatever natives they could capture. As the slave trade grew, however, such hit-or-miss methods were no longer feasible. The cooperation of the native rulers was secured and these sold their fellow Africans to the slavers. Large-scale Negro slavery became possible only through the cooperation of Negro leaders.

Companies engaged in the slave trade established posts along the coast where their representatives bought slaves either directly from native rulers or from middlemen. The slaves were kept temporarily in enclosures called barracoons until they could be exported. Captains of slave ships might also bargain for slaves directly. The native rulers secured the slaves whom they were to sell in various ways. But because the most common way was to capture them in war, one of the many evil effects of the trade was the encouragement of internecine strife.

As the trade increased, sources of supply near the coast began to be exhausted, and slaves had to be brought from farther and farther inland. They were transported in coffles, that is, in lines of captives marching in single file, each being tied by the neck to the one in front and the one behind. It seems probable that some of these coffles were marched as far as five hundred miles before reaching the coast. The whole process was incredibly cruel and incredibly costly in human life. Few details are known; for few white men penetrated into the interior to observe and report this aspect of the slave trade. It involved the psychological shock of capture, the sudden and forced separation from family, friends, and home, and a dangerous and physically exhausting journey to the coast. Just how many deaths all this involved can only be guessed. Daniel P. Mannix estimates that the total number of slaves exported from Africa to all countries during the four centuries of the slave trade amounted to some fifteen million and that, in addition, the trade caused "the death of perhaps thirty or forty million others in slave raids, coffles, and barracoons."[5] As stated, this is only a guess, although it is the guess of an expert. However, the statement does bring out one gruesome fact. Even before the slaves were put aboard ship, a large toll in human lives had been taken which probably amounted to something of the order of two or three deaths for every exported slave.

The details of the Middle Passage form one of the most hideous chapters in the whole history of human cruelty. At best a voyage by sail of from three weeks to three months through tropical waters was a trying experience. In the slave ships it was appalling. The slaves had to face overcrowding, lack of sanitation, and the constant threat of disease. Captains and crews were extraordinarily callous. The slaves were bewildered and desperate. Many simply lost the desire to live. Prevention of suicide was a constant problem for their captors.

The efficient use of cargo space was one among many details debated by captains of slave ships. There were two schools of thought among these economic theoreticians. One school, the "loose-packers," argued that if the slaves were allowed a reasonable amount of space and given fairly good treatment there would be fewer deaths during the voyage and the survivors would be in better physical condition and would therefore bring better prices upon arrival. On the other hand, the "tight-packers" held that although overcrowding did indeed increase mortality, they would be more than compensated for this loss by the greater net profits from a larger cargo, and if the slaves arrived in poor physical condition they could be "fattened up" in a slave yard in the West Indies before sale.

It is incredible to learn just how extreme the policies of the tight-packers were. During a Parliamentary investigation in 1788 a Captain Parrey of the Royal Navy was sent to Liverpool to measure the slave ships lying in port there. What he found may be illustrated by conditions on the *Brookes,* a ship which he considered typical. On this ship a space six feet long, by sixteen inches wide, and usually about thirty-one inches high was allowed for an adult man, with correspondingly smaller spaces for women and children. As someone remarked during the same Parliamentary investigation, a coffin would have been more roomy. During fair weather slaves were brought on deck and exercised at intervals. During stormy weather, this was impossible and the suffering of the slaves packed together in the intense heat was unbearable.

The ruthlessness of some of the captains of the slave ships is equally hard to believe. An extreme case is that of the *Zong* out of Liverpool which sailed from São Thomé for Jamaica in 1781 with a white crew of 17 men and a cargo of 440 slaves. The passage was slow and there was a great deal of sickness. Seven seamen and more than sixty slaves died. The remaining slaves were so weakened that their market value was doubtful. In the meantime, the supply of fresh water ran short and it appeared that there would not be enough for the rest of the trip. Therefore, the captain decided to throw overboard the weakest slaves, arguing that this would be legal jettison covered by insurance, whereas

34

deaths from illness or thirst would not be covered. The order was actually carried out and 132 slaves were jettisoned. The case became known to the public only because the underwriters refused to pay insurance on the jettisoned slaves and the shipowners brought the case into court. The decision eventually handed down was in favor of the underwriters. Yet the very fact that the justification of the captain's action could be seriously debated in a court of law projects a clear light on the low state of the public conscience at this time.[6]

After landing, the slaves had to be "seasoned" before they could be sold to planters; that is, they had to learn the language of their future masters, to learn a new etiquette, and to familiarize themselves with the tools and processes of an unfamiliar system of agriculture. Above all, any latent tendency towards revolt had to be extinguished in them. Only then, broken in spirit and ready for work, could they be sold. For obvious reasons, the mortality during the seasoning period was high.

The quality of treatment which the slaves received has long been a highly controversial subject. While the abolitionists represented slavery as unmitigated horror, apologists for the system painted a picture of idyllic contentment. Undoubtedly, there was much variation, and no doubt sometimes there was real affection between slave and master. There is evidence that some wealthy slaveowners liked to pamper their household servants.[7] On the other hand, it is equally verifiable that some slaveowners were sadists, and some were psychopaths who abused their slaves in the most perverse ways. In addition to differences in treatment traceable to their masters, there were differences that stemmed from the work assigned to the slaves. There were field hands and domestic servants; some were highly skilled workmen; and a few worked on railroads, on ships, or in factories. All this makes generalization difficult.

But the one principle that unquestionably determined the master-slave relationship was that of economics. Slaves had been imported for the precise purpose of serving as productive laborers. Because slavery did not fit into the economy of the northern states, as we have already noted, it soon died out there. Because it did fit into the economy of the plantation, it flourished wherever plantations flourished. The slave was legally defined as a chattel. Like his owner's fields and barns, his tools and farm animals, the slave was an essential element in a complex scheme of profit making. This fact remained the overriding, inescapable fact, whatever feeling a master might have towards his slave as a human being.

On reasonably well-run plantations slaves probably received fairly good care, but only for the same reasons that farm animals did also. If a horse was ailing, a veterinarian was called; if a slave was ailing, a physician was called.[8] It was nothing more than short-sighted economic policy to overwork a slave or a mule to the point of permanently injuring one or the other's efficiency. It was a rudimentary truism: underfed cows do not produce a normal quantity of good milk, and underfed slaves did not produce a normal quantity of good work. Apologists for slavery were perhaps not wholly wrong when they boasted that slaves received good physical care. By today's standards their treatment was perhaps atrocious; but by the standards of contemporary free

36

workers in northern factories it was probably not altogether dreadful.

Modern students of slavery are beginning to realize that the real horror of the system lay not in the physical cruelties it imposed, but in psychological factors relating to the complete subjugation of slave to master.[9] Every plantation was a miniature totalitarian state. The planter made whatever laws suited him and enforced them by his own arbitrary penal code. He might whip refractory slaves, and whip them cruelly, or he might put them in the stocks, lock them up in a private or public jail, give them extra tasks, demote them to less desirable jobs, employ the services of a professional slave-breaker, or sell them to some distant plantation.[10] It was reasonably safe to kill a slave. Legally, it might be murder, but conviction was difficult because Negroes—the most likely witnesses—were not allowed to testify against a white person, because the law recognized many extenuating circumstances, and because white juries were simply very reluctant to convict.[11]

For the average person, marriage and family life answer fundamental emotional needs. For the slave, anything resembling normal family life was very difficult, if not impossible. Neither marriage nor fatherhood among slaves had any legal status. To live together, a couple of course needed the master's consent; then there might, or might not, be some sort of a marriage ceremony. Divorce, like marriage, was entirely within the master's discretion. Although public sentiment was against it, there were only weak legal restrictions against the breakup of families by sale.[12] The slave family had almost no social significance. The mother was a full-time worker for her owner; she usually had little time

37

to devote to her children and only such authority over them as her owner allowed. Man and wife usually worked apart in separate labor gangs. The husband and father was not the head of the family. He might be forced to stand by, helpless and humiliated, while his wife was disrobed and whipped before his eyes; and he had no redress whatever if his wife were raped by the plantation owner or his sons.

Even the slave's religious life was under his master's control. Of course, it was only with the owner's permission that slaves could leave the plantation to attend church or that a clergyman could come on it to minister to the slaves. A common policy was to encourage religion among slaves, but to see to it that they would be taught only a harmless version of Christianity in which the duty of obedience was stressed. Sometimes slaves were allowed to hold their own religious services, but then the owner or an overseer would attend, and naturally the slave who was allowed to play the role of clergyman would not be one with subversive tendencies.

The slave's liberty was restricted in numberless ways. He did not have freedom of movement; the usual practice was to require him to have a pass whenever he left his home plantation. Unlike the freeman, he had no liberty to choose his occupation or his place of residence. It was illegal to teach slaves to read and write; and if a few of them circumvented this prohibition, it was only due to an almost superhuman persistence. Slaves even dressed in whatever clothes their masters gave them, and would amuse themselves only as their masters approved.

Just how the human spirit was crushed by slavery has been illustrated by the testimony of former slaves. For example, Frederick Douglass thus describes his reaction to the system at one period of his life: "I was broken in body, soul, and spirit. My natural elasticity was crushed, my intellect languished, the disposition to read departed, the cheerful spark that lingered about my eye died; the dark night of slavery closed in upon me; and behold a man transformed into a brute!"[13] Douglass was a young man at the time and possessed of extraordinary intelligence, courage, and will. As is well known, he eventually threw off this mood, escaped from slavery, and became a national figure. Most slaves were far less resilient. For the most part, they were driven into a childish servility or an animal-like apathy, without ambition and without hope. Such was, indeed, "the dark night of slavery."

It is hard to find elsewhere a parallel to the psychological effect of American Negro slavery. Conditions in Latin America were not similar; for there slaves had some definite rights which were safeguarded.[14] Nor does prison life today offer an accurate parallel, for while incarceration can break a man's spirit—and some prisoners do develop psychoses—a guard's authority over a prisoner is strictly regulated. Even in maximum-security prisons there does not exist that total subjugation of one man to another's whim that existed on the plantation.

Probably the closest parallel to plantation slavery is furnished by the German concentration camps. In one respect, it is clear, the two situations were vastly different. The SS men deliberately maltreated their captives and put them to death with indifference, whereas the slaves, in the eyes of the slaveholders, were valuable property which they were reluctant to damage in any permanent way. Yet in both cases there was the feature of total power, and the captives' reaction to it in the camp and on the plantation was surprisingly similar. Concentration-camp inmates, we are told, developed childish forms of behavior. Even more surprisingly, they tended to see in the SS man a father symbol, and learned not to hate him in spite of his cruelty. All this sounds familiar: the patriarchal slaveholder and his childlike slaves are common-places of plantation literature.[15]

From first to last, the slave trade and American slavery were diabolically evil. Yet the system was supported not only by decent and respectable citizens, but by men of heroic mold. Americans are justly proud of the great leaders who created their nation "conceived in liberty and dedicated to the proposition that all men are created equal." Yet, as we know, such truly noble men as Washington and Jefferson were slaveholders. They had their moments of uneasiness and compunction, they dreamed of eventual emancipation—but they kept their slaves.[16]

In the decades before the Civil War, the South produced many outstanding statesmen; but the genius of these men—comparable to that of certain southern Senators today—was mobilized not only to oppose immediate emancipation, but to oppose anything that would weaken the slavery system. Moreover, they even fought to spread slavery into the new territories that were being opened up in the West, and finally and tragically they fought for these ends so stubbornly that they were willing to bring on civil war rather than compromise. Yet these men did not appear to be fanatics. On the contrary, they were for the most part sober, intelligent, reasonable, often warmhearted men of broad human sympathy.

The attitudes of the churches were rather complex.[17] Here there will be space to consider only Catholics and slavery.[18] Not only did Catholic lay people own slaves, but so also did religious communities, including at least Jesuits, Capuchins, and Dominicans, as well as Ursuline and Carmelite nuns.[19] There were slaves at the school founded by Father Dubois at Emmitsburg.[20] Archbishop Carroll was a slaveholder.[21] Religious communities not only bought and sold slaves,[22] they also leased them out.[23] Moreover, these religious did not use slaves exclusively for personal service or for the cultivation of necessary food to be used by the community; the religious communities also engaged in plantation agriculture *for a profit*.[24] Roger Baudier observes a Jesuit plantation in the middle years of the eighteenth century: "The plantation at New Orleans had developed into quite a prosperous establishment with a constant increase in the number of buildings and slaves on the large tract of land that faced the river and extended back towards the cypress swamp. The revenues from this plantation helped to defray the expenses of the distant Jesuit missions of the province."[25]

Nor was the Catholic hierarchy very outspoken in criticism of slavery. In the South, where Catholics were a small minority and where pro-slavery pressure was intense, the bishops tended to conform to the local mores. Madeleine Rice concludes, after a thorough study, that in the South "the chief emphasis was given to the acceptance of the system by scriptural and church author-

41

ity—with emancipation as a very remote possibility."[26] This was the doctrine that Bishop England had made popular.

In the North, Catholics were somewhat more inclined to look on eventual freedom as the solution of the slavery question, but they remained strongly opposed to the abolitionists who advocated immediate emancipation. This was in part because abolitionism was looked on as a radical movement with links to secular and anticlerical European revolutionaries. A great many Catholics were Democrats, and this influenced them in the direction of a states-rights attitude with its attendant weak opposition to slavery. Catholic unskilled laborers, a large group, feared the competition of emancipated Negroes. Here as elsewhere, economics crushed morality.

In the discussion that immediately preceded the Emancipation Proclamation, northern Catholics were divided. Archbishop Hughes of New York was their most prominent spokesman. In his debates with the layman Orestes Brownson, he adopted a pro-slavery position and declared—in fairly characteristic rhetoric—that abolitionists who advocated immediate emancipation needed "the humane protection of a lunatic asylum." Although condemning the slave trade in the abstract, he justified the American trade on account of particular circumstances. He said that if Catholics in the war "are to fight for the abolition of slavery, then indeed they will turn away in disgust from the discharge of what would otherwise be a patriotic duty." Of course, Archbishop Hughes represented an extreme position. However, he had many sympathizers, and it is significant that this prelate who was widely regarded as the spokesman for northern Catholics could have taken a pro-slavery position.[27]

How is it, one must inquire, that an evil as grievous as American slavery could be condoned not only by average decent and respectable citizens, not only by politicians, but by many leaders of the Church as well? The dead weight of custom is, no doubt, part of the answer. A long-standing practice embodied in law is assumed by most persons to be just. In the case of slavery there were, moreover, a number of standard rationalizations so often repeated that they were widely accepted as valid. One of these was the argument that both Scripture and Church doctrine sanctioned slavery.

Catholic teaching on slavery probably differed little from the consensus of the Western world. The subject is complex but for the present purpose what is relevant can be summarized briefly. First, it must be admitted that slavery loosely defined is not in itself opposed to the moral law in all possible cases. Life imprisonment as a punishment is actually a very extreme form of slavery and it can be justified. More than that, if one man can sell his labor to another for, say, a year, there is no reason why he cannot sell it for life in return for adequate food, clothing, and shelter. Slavery in this sense, the sale of one's labor in perpetuity, can be justified; but it is important to realize that it is only labor that can be sold. The bondsman must retain his fundamental human rights, such as his right to family life and his right to practice his religion; in a word, he retains all rights except the right to revoke his labor contract without his master's consent. Furthermore, there must be adequate safeguards for these rights. In a pre-money economy, the exchange of lifetime labor for lifetime physical care could be a practical arrangement; at least it is not obviously unjust in itself. It must be added, however, that history shows that even the most benign forms of slavery have seldom proved just in practice.[28]

But these abstract considerations have little relation to the sordid facts of American Negro slavery. We have quoted Mannix to the effect that for every slave exported from Africa, two or three others died in slave raids, coffles, or barracoons. The English Privy Council in 1789 estimated that of the slaves exported from Africa, 12½ per cent died in the Middle Passage, 4½ per cent died while the slave ships were in harbor, and another 33 per cent died during the seasoning process, a total of 50 per cent.[29] Thus it may be estimated that for every two slaves exported from Africa, about five had already died and that, of these two, one would die before the other was sold to a planter. If these figures are correct, the sale of a slave in America cost six deaths. These figures are estimates and may not be entirely accurate, but even so, it is impossible to doubt the central fact that for every slave sold in America several others had died. The one man who survived was sold into such an inhuman existence that he might well envy the others. Whatever might be said of slavery in the abstract, to justify the murderous and inhuman American slave system as it in fact existed required self-deception of grotesque proportions.

But would it be deception if the slave were *truly* inferior, were by nature as well as by law a mere chattel? This insidious rationalization attempted to justify slavery on the ground that the special psychological make-up of the Negro's personality made slavery advantageous for him. A classic example of this theory is to be found in a treatise by George Fitzhugh published in 1854

44

and curiously titled *Sociology for the South*.[30] According to Fitzhugh, the Negro "is but a grown up child." Just as it is right that
white children should be under the strict control of their parents
until maturity, so it is right that the Negro, who is a perpetual
child, should perpetually be under the strict control of his master.
"The Negro race is inferior." Therefore, if the slaves were to be
emancipated, they could never survive in a competitive culture
with the whites. "Gradual but certain extermination would be
their fate." Emancipation would be cruel.[31]

One reason why ante-bellum apologists could hold such views
was the fact that they were profoundly ignorant of the culture of
West Africa where most of the slaves were captured. Although
the complexity of this culture makes generalization difficult, it is
unquestionably safe to say that it was an agricultural economy
with settled cities and villages. The West Africans were "food
producers" and thus represented a more advanced stage of cultural evolution than, for example, the North American Indians
who were, for the most part, nomadic "food gatherers." The soil
and climate of West Africa were such that farming required a
great deal of toil and self-discipline. The economy was intricately
organized with a high degree of division of labor. An elaborate
system of rules and customs governed trade. Political institutions
were developed to the point that some native states were large
and had very stable governments with elaborate systems of law
and courts. In a word, the picture of West African life painted by
anthropological research is poles apart from the crude savagery
imagined by the apologists for slavery.[32]

There is a cruel unconscious irony in the fact that the slaveholder—and his heirs—have blamed the Negroes for conditions

which they themselves had created. The slaveholder denied slaves the right to hold property and then blamed them for being improvident. He denied them the right to education and then blamed them for being stupid. He denied them the possibility of rising above a servile condition and then blamed them for lacking ambition. He took from the slaves all possibility of the exercise of initiative and then blamed them for being childishly dependent.

Modern research has failed to demonstrate the existence of any inherited interracial differences of personality or ability between Negroes and whites. There are formidable difficulties in research on these topics. Human behavior is constantly, fundamentally, and intimately influenced by the social environment. To strip away the effect of this environment and to compare the native endowments which newborn infants of different races bring with them into the world is difficult almost to the point of impossibility. Up to the present, the best that the modern behavioral sciences can do on the question of inborn psychological differences among the races is to bring in the verdict of "not proven."[33]

Still another rationalization was based on the claim that the slaves were content with their condition. No injustice was done by withholding a freedom which they did not desire. In support of this contention, instances were adduced of slaves who were offered emancipation and refused it.

It is true that slaves occasionally refused emancipation, but such instances were very exceptional. Moreover, in the occasional instances of refusal there were usually compelling reasons why

46

acceptance was not feasible. Emancipation regularly carried with it the proviso that the freed slave should leave his home state for some other state or even that he should migrate to Liberia.[34] He might not have the money needed for travel, and in any case he would have to leave his friends, probably his family, and try to earn his living in a strange new environment. Moreover, the status of the free Negro was itself an underprivileged status. The circumstances being what they were, it is perhaps not surprising that emancipation was not always accepted.

There is undeniable evidence that the great majority of slaves hated slavery. If they had been contented with the system, one may suppose that they would have cheerfully cooperated with it. As a matter of fact, they didn't: the plantation literature is full of complaints about the way the slaves, unless they were constantly supervised, would slow the pace of their labor, work carelessly, damage property, try to escape their tasks by malingering, engage in petty theft, and harass their owners and overseers in numerous other subtle and ingenious ways. Kenneth Stampp remarks that the slaves most prone to such behavior "were the meek, smiling ones whom many thought were contented though irresponsible."[35] Their contentment, apparently, was not very deep.

A similar indicator of discontent was furnished by the "runaways" who fled from their servitude even though escape was difficult and hazardous. A system of slave patrols watched out for stray slaves who could not show the required pass from their masters. A captured fugitive was severely punished. Even if he escaped to free territory, he might still be brought back to servitude under fugitive slave legislation. Yet the desire for freedom

47

was so intense that many fled in spite of all difficulties. A southern judge estimated in 1855 that more than sixty thousand slaves had gained freedom in the North up to that date, and this was probably a conservative figure.[36]

A final proof of the slaves' deep-rooted discontent is furnished by the slave revolts. It is hard to determine just how many of these occurred. There were large and dramatic cases such as Gabriel's Conspiracy of 1800 or that of Denmark Vesey in 1822. Most striking of all was Nat Turner's Rebellion of 1831. At the other extreme there were many small revolts which were hardly more than instances of individual violence. Perhaps the safest conclusion is that of Ulrich Phillips, who states that enough plots were discovered and enough revolts actually occurred "to maintain a fairly constant undertone of uneasiness."[37] This chronic uneasiness among the slaveholders betrayed their consciousness of a chronic discontent among the slaves.

For a successful revolt against the iniquitous mores of a paramoral society, the individual needs two things. He needs a factual knowledge of existing conditions; and he needs moral principles applicable to those conditions. In the days of American Negro slavery, both factual knowledge and moral principles were in short supply.

At the time of the Emancipation Proclamation the behavioral sciences were virtually nonexistent. Anthropology could give no insights into the complexities of West African culture; psychology had nothing valid to say about comparative racial make-up; sociology could throw no light on the reactions of the individual to his social environment under the very special conditions of chattel slavery. Yet, even though science was of no assistance, it is distressing that intelligent men could have remained so blind to the obvious facts of the situation that they could seriously have believed that the slaves were contented with their state, or that they were so markedly different from other human beings that slavery was not only compatible with but apropos of their nature. The progress of scientific research should not be required to disabuse men of such obvious errors. A simple willingness to face the facts should be enough.

Even those who recognized the intrinsic or at least the circumstantial evil of slavery could not bring moral principles to bear. It is incongruous, and indeed more than incongruous, that priests and bishops could have dedicated their lives, as they actually did, to the generous service of their neighbor in charity and yet have remained unaware, ineptly and rudely unaware, of the inhuman evils of slavery.

The general principles of charity and justice were not in undue need of clarification. The popes had condemned the slave trade and the evils of slavery in general. Yet the principle of conformity to the prevalent mores carried the day. A theology of disobedience was never developed.

3

The Slaughter of the European Jews

SLAVERY has died out in all but a few small isolated regions, and with its passing one might have hoped that the moral callousness it evinced was also becoming a thing of record. Were there ever such a hope, and no doubt there was, unfortunately no one could have known as well as the man of today how foolish it was. Mere slavery has been superseded. Mass murder has become the hallmark of twentieth-century man's inhumanity to man.

Some 5,100,000 European Jews—Polish, German, French, Czechs, Slovaks—were slaughtered under Hitler.[1] This genocidal act was probably not, however, the vastest mass murder of our time. Millions of Armenians and Greeks lost their lives under the Turkish persecution of 1914–15, Stalin's great purge of 1937–38 was extremely bloody,[2] and millions of persons were put to death in Communist China. Millions more, combatants and noncombatants, were slain in the two world wars. Wholesale killing is characteristic of our century.

The basic reason for studying here the Nazi persecution of the Jews, out of all these bloodbaths, is that its horrors are so very well documented. With the fall of Germany the Allies captured most of the confidential archives of all branches of the government. "Never before, I believe," writes William Shirer, "has such a vast treasure fallen into the hands of contemporary historians."[3]

It is this documentation which makes the study of the paramoral society of Nazi Germany so illuminating.

Of course, it is impossible to comprehend the monstrosity of a crime consisting of more than five million murders. One may perhaps, to some extent, grasp the enormous evil of a single murder. Readers of Anne Frank's diary, when they reflect on the killing of this charming and innocent teen-ager, have shared a revulsion, a sense of horror, at the utter cruelty of this deed.[4] However, when we multiply this deed by ten thousand, by a hundred thousand, by five million, we enter a region where the human imagination simply gives out. It is totally impossible to realize the magnitude of the crime committed against the European Jews.

Before the Jews were persecuted, they first had to be defined; for even the most ardent anti-Semites are not always sure precisely who it is they hate.[5] In Hitler's Germany, after a good deal of discussion among the philosophers of persecution, a law of November 14, 1935, defined as a Jew any person with either four or three Jewish grandparents. Those with two Jewish grandparents were also included if they belonged to the Jewish religion, or were married to a Jewish person before September 15, 1935. The balance of those with two Jewish grandparents and all those with one Jewish grandparent were defined as *Mischlinge,* that is, half bloods.[6] In general, the *Mischlinge* were not persecuted, but they did suffer some relatively minor restrictions: in order to marry Germans, they needed official approval; they could not enter the civil service or the party; and in the army they could not rise above the rank of private.

The campaign against the Jews can be roughly divided into

51

two periods. From the Nazi accession to power in 1933 up to the summer of 1941, there was a period of harassment. During this time Jews were saddled with increasingly severe disabilities. This eliminated them from the German power structure and induced a great many to emigrate. Soon after the 1941 invasion of the U.S.S.R. a new policy was adopted and a period of annihilation began which ended only with the collapse of the Third Reich. These two periods of harassment (1933–41) and annihilation (1941–45) will be considered separately, though it should be emphasized that the two periods overlapped. Many Jews were put to death before the annihilation policy was formally adopted and new methods of harassment continued to be introduced up to the very end.

The persecution began even before the official definition of the term "Jew" was promulgated. Very soon after Hitler came to power Jews were gradually eliminated from the civil service. They were not allowed to serve as newspaper editors. Jewish artists, writers, and musicians were forbidden to practice their professions. In private business the matter was somewhat more complicated. Some firms were owned by Jews and in others they held positions of skill and experience in which they would be hard to replace. However, as a result of constant pressure and a complicated series of laws and decrees, Jews were gradually eliminated from the business sector. Under the stress of this persecution many Jews, not surprisingly, decided to emigrate. Through a flight tax and through exchange controls almost all the property of the emigrants was confiscated.

As time went on the persecution was intensified. In 1938 Jewish relief organizations lost their tax exemption; and soon after Jews were excluded in principle from the public relief rolls. When a minor official at the German Embassy in Paris was killed by a Jewish assassin on November 9, 1938, the Nazi government retaliated by levying a special "atonement payment" (*Sühneleistung*), a tax of 20 per cent (later increased to 25 per cent) on all registered property of Jews. In addition, income-tax policies began to be applied selectively against them. Tax exemptions for Jewish children were abolished, and finally, in 1940, a special income tax for Jews was instituted.

By 1939 the Jewish community had shrunk to half its original size; and the emigration of the able-bodied had left it with a disproportionate number of aged persons for whom self-support was difficult. Moreover, expropriations and discriminatory hiring policies had deprived of their ordinary means of support even the more capable among those remaining. In 1939 unemployed Jews were conscripted for forced labor on reclamation and construction projects. Jews still working for private employers also had to suffer. On October 4, 1941, Jews were assigned a separate labor status by a decree which deprived them of all the protection which modern labor laws usually grant employees. Extreme exploitation of Jewish workers was thus facilitated.

During the period of the war, food shortages were often quite acute. It is not surprising that, in line with current Nazi policy, food regulations were used as an additional means of harassing the Jews. Authorities began with comparatively mild measures, such as depriving Jews of special allotments or assigning them special shopping hours so that non-Jews would have first choice of available food. Gradually, the discrimination became more and more extreme until in 1942 doctors were forbidden to prescribe any sort of supplementary rations for Jewish patients, milk rations for Jewish children were cut drastically, and supplementary rations were denied to Jewish night workers, extra-hour workers, and workers with unusually laborious tasks. Thus starvation became an additional weapon in Hitler's arsenal.

Another of these weapons constantly used against the Jews during the period of harassment deserves special discussion. This is what may be called the regular or ordinary concentration camp in contrast to the extermination camps (*Vernichtungslager*) which will be described later and which played the most tragic role during the period of Jewish annihilation.[7] Prisoners in the regular camps included a great many categories beside Jews. Most numerous were the political prisoners ranging from Communists to conscientious objectors and Jehovah's Witnesses. In addition, there was an equally wide variety of "asocial" individuals, habitual criminals, vagrants, homosexuals, alcoholics, and others. Some were interned so that the regime might extort money from them; some were sent to camp to satisfy the personal hatred of important party officials.

As one may gather from the character of the camps' population, their principal purpose was to eliminate from the community everyone who had opposed Nazi policies and to create an atmosphere of terror which would prevent others from following their example. However, there were certain subordinate purposes. The camps were a reliable source of cheap labor, and they served as a training school for Hitler's Blackshirts, members of the SS (*Schutzstaffel*). For them the camps provided a graduate course in cruelty. Finally, when the extermination camps were opened, they furnished subjects for medical experiments.

The earliest concentration camps appeared soon after Hitler came to power. Probably there were fifty by the end of 1933, but they were small. As time went on, the trend was towards larger and more formally organized camps, among which Dachau, Buchenwald, Sachsenhausen, and Ravensbrück (for women) were specially infamous. Figures on the subject are unreliable, but it seems that the larger camps at this time had 20,000 inmates or more; but with the outbreak of war there was a great expansion. It has been estimated that in the period 1943–45 there were about twenty large camps, each with some 25,000 inmates, in addition to many smaller camps.[8] At one time or another, perhaps almost eight million persons were imprisoned; there may have been about 700,000 survivors.[9]

It was a regular policy to treat camp inmates with deliberate cruelty. They were starved, overworked, inadequately clad, deprived of necessary sleep, and given very meager medical attention. They were whipped and beaten for the most trifling violations of complicated rules. Punishment might take the form of fatigue drill lasting for hours. It is not surprising that the death rate in the regular camps (not the extermination camps) never fell below 10 per cent per year and was often much higher.[10] Bruno Bettelheim remarks that the death rate was particularly high among new prisoners, perhaps as high as 15 per cent per *month* during the first months; but as the prisoner learned to adjust to camp life, death rates fell sharply.[11]

Devastating as were the physical effects of camp life, the psychological effects were perhaps even worse. There was first the shock of arrest itself, of being suddenly torn away from family and friends and ordinary occupations and being placed in confinement without any possibility of legal redress. Moreover, during transportation from the place of arrest to the camp, which lasted at least twelve hours, SS men systematically tortured the prisoners by whipping, kicking, shooting, or stabbing with the bayonet. Extreme exhaustion was deliberately produced by forcing prisoners to kneel for hours or to stare into glaring lights. SS men humiliated the prisoners further by forcing them to violate their most cherished principles by accusing themselves and one another of every conceivable vile action.

In camp the dependence of the inmate on the SS guards was absolute. He was entirely at the guard's mercy. Every detail of his life, even permission to visit the latrine, was completely at the discretion of the guard. There was no privacy, no possibility of modesty—a situation particularly degrading for the women inmates.[12] As a result of all this some prisoners lost the will to live and became, as it were, walking corpses.[13] Others, as we have noted, developed a childlike dependence on the SS guards who assumed the role of father figures. Only the exceptional person was able to retain that secret inner independence which made survival possible. Perhaps the ultimate cruelty of the camp system was that so many of those who were executed could not die as heroes; often it was as whimpering children that they met death.

As we have said, the regular type of camp, now being discussed, was used for a great variety of persons beside Jews. However, the Jews were particularly vulnerable. A gentile, if he was careful constantly to appear docile and inoffensive, had no reason to fear being sent to the camps. A Jew had no such assurance. Moreover, in the camps themselves, Jews were regularly singled out for especially harsh treatment. Thus, even before the period of the "final solution," the camps played a large role in the persecution of the Jews.

In the summer of 1941 the period of harassment merged into the period of annihilation. What had long been implicit in Nazi doctrine now became explicit policy. All Jews within the German sphere of influence were to be rounded up and killed. For this purpose two different methods were used. First, there were the mobile units which sought out groups of Jews and killed them on the spot. Secondly, there were the extermination camps to which Jews were transported. By the first method, the killers went to their victims; by the second, the victims were brought to their killers. We will now discuss these two types of murder separately.

When the German army attacked the U.S.S.R. on June 22, 1941, it was accompanied by small mobile killing units. All in all, the latter had a total strength of about 3,000 men. These units were responsible to the Reich Security Main Office (*Reichssicherheitshauptamt*), an amalgamation of state police and party personnel which maintained control over the units with much efficiency. For the operation of these units, Army assistance was necessary, and there was at first some doubt as to whether this would be forthcoming. The fear proved groundless. The cooperation of army officials left nothing to be desired.

The details of the killing operation varied according to time and circumstance. In the earlier stages, Jews were often deceived into compliance by ruse; later more brute force had to be used. In any case, a town would be selected where there was a concentration of Jews and a mass grave was dug at some secluded spot near it. The actual execution would perhaps begin at night, but more often near dawn. Jews were ordered to assemble at some point; those who did not were sought out and brought by force. Then they were transported by truck to the killing site. There they might be lined up on the edge of the grave and shot; whereupon they toppled in. An alternative was the "sardine method" (*Ölsardinenmanier*). A first group would be made to lie down side by side at the bottom of the grave. These would be shot. Then another group would be made to lie down on top of the dead, their heads at the corpses' feet. After five or six layers, the grave would be filled in. Even the more brutalized executioners found their task distasteful, and therefore often reported for duty very intoxicated—and for this reason did not always work efficiently. Sometimes victims remained alive a whole night, bleeding and suffering; or they might even manage to crawl away alive, usually to be captured later and killed.[14]

These murder units accounted for about 1,400,000 Jewish deaths or somewhat more than a quarter of the total; the balance died in extermination camps, which thus constituted the most usual method of killing.[15] Like the mobile killing units, the extermination camps were responsible to an agency of the party bureaucracy. After February 1, 1942, nearly all the camps were directly or indirectly under the control of the Economic-Administrative Main Office (*Wirtschafts-Verwaltungshauptamt*).[16] It is important to note that all murder operations were thus under civilian bureaucratic agencies.

Some of the camps, such as Kulmhof or Belzec, were extermination centers only; other camps were partly labor camps. Those Jews who were too weak for work on arrival were killed forthwith, but the others were worked until they became too feeble to be useful. The work performed included camp maintenance, camp construction, and certain enterprises under SS control, for example the gravel works at Auschwitz and Treblinka, or the cement works at Mauthausen and Lublin. In addition to all this, private industry contracted to use camp labor. Thus I. G. Farben, the great German chemical firm, established factories at Auschwitz for the manufacture of acetic acid and synthetic rubber. Later Krupp opened a fuse plant there. Other companies followed suit.[17] It is significant that highly respected business men cooperated fully with the SS in the exploitation of Jews at the extermination camps.

Methods of killing varied from camp to camp. Sometimes execution was by shooting; but at the larger camps gas vans or, more commonly, permanent gas chambers were used. The usual lethal agent was carbon monoxide (CO), but at Auschwitz the more efficient hydrogen cyanide (HCN) was used. Bodies were disposed of by being buried, cremated in ovens, or burned in open pits.

Similarly, the murder process differed from camp to camp. The following was the routine at Auschwitz which was the largest of the extermination centers. Since this camp was in part a labor camp, the first step was to select those fit for work. New arrivals were marched in front of a camp doctor who indicated each victim's fate by a flick of his thumb. "Left" meant immediate death. "Right" meant a labor assignment. Of course, those in the latter category gained only a temporary reprieve; they lived in constant terror of the inevitable decision which would send them also to the gas chambers.

Those sent to the left had first to give up their luggage. Then the sexes were separated, and the victims were marched to the gas chambers, still unaware of their fate. Sometimes an orchestra played to create a deceptive mood of relaxation. On arriving at the gas chambers, the doomed were still not terrified; for signs indicated that these were baths and disinfection rooms. Then they had to take off their clothes. The women's hair was cut off, since this valuable commodity could be used, for example, to make felt shoes for U-boat men. Then the victims were crowded into the gas chambers. If at last their suspicions were aroused, SS men drove them in with rods and whips.

Once the door was closed, lights were turned off. Then the SS man, wearing a gas mask emptied cans of HCN pellets into the chamber. Panic ensued, as the victims struggled for a breath of the diminishing air. In two minutes all was silence. In four minutes everyone was dead. At other camps, where CO was used, the agony might last as long as three hours. Finally, the doors were thrown open and the unpleasant task of removing the bodies and cleaning up the chamber was performed by special Jewish work squads, *Sonderkommandos,* whose members were regularly executed, to be succeeded by new squads.

It is our thesis that the major crimes of history are committed with the cooperation of the type of citizen usually described as decent and respectable. This was eminently true in the case of the destruction of the European Jews. Raul Hilberg writes: "However one may wish to draw the line of active participation, the machinery of destruction was a remarkable cross-section of the German population. Every profession, every skill, and every social status was represented in it."[18]

If this is to be understood in the sense that those who shot and gassed the Jews were a simple random sample of the German population, it is probably an exaggeration. The extermination camps were manned by SS men and they seem to have been a unique social type. They were not, indeed, a homogeneous group. Some were "sadists in the purest clinical sense," but at the other extreme some were humane.[19] However, it is a reasonable conjecture to say that the modal type of SS man was that which is to be found in the extremist fringe of most social movements, the type of person who compensates for personal feelings of inferiority by identifying himself with some dramatic group of social insurgents.

Whatever the character of the rank and file, the executives who had charge of the extermination process had to be reliable, efficient, and "capable" people. Speaking of the leaders of the mobile killing operations, Hilberg says: "These men were in no sense hoodlums, delinquents, common criminals, or sex maniacs. Most were intellectuals."[20] Thus Ohlendorf had been a research scientist; Biberstein, a pastor; Weinmann, a physician; Klingelhöfer, a professional opera singer. In the extermination camps, too, a good proportion of the leaders were career men in the civil service who had drawn that particular assignment. "All necessary operations," writes Hilberg, "were accomplished with whatever personnel were at hand."[21]

After the war, many of those actively concerned in the killing operations escaped detection and settled down in civilian life. Some of these were conspicuously successful, and if they were later arrested, they usually proved to be good examples of what one can only call "decent and respectable citizens." A prime example is Ewald Peters, who became department chief of the West

61

German secret service. He was a refined man, devoted to art and music, personally rather shy and modest. In his capacity as a security officer he had accompanied Chancellor Erhard on official visits and had met President Johnson, President De Gaulle, and Pope Paul. Yet evidence finally turned up that this mild and efficient civil servant had served as a platoon commander in one of the mobile killing units and had taken part in the slaughter of 12,000 Ukrainian Jews. He was arrested as a war criminal and committed suicide in his cell.

The efficient operation of both the mobile killing units and the extermination camps required the active cooperation of other agencies until practically all segments of the German power structure were involved. The wholehearted cooperation of the army with the mobile killing units has already been mentioned. The business world was also involved; the operations of I. G. Farben, Krupp, and smaller firms at Auschwitz have been noted. In addition to this, various companies were eager for contracts to construct gas chambers and crematoria, as well as to furnish the quantities of HCN required for gassing. Physicians were willing to cooperate in atrocious medical experiments. Finally, responsibility had to be shared by wide sectors of the government bureaucracy if the extermination centers were to be efficiently run. Prisoners had to be transported to the camps by the tens of thousands and this involved elaborate railroad scheduling. Food had to be provided, and this added up to a great deal of food for the large number of camp inmates, even though they received only a starvation diet. There was a complicated system of disposing of inmates' effects which included the shipping of dental gold to the Reichsbank. The flow of money which all this involved had to be followed by government accountants. The capture and transportation of Jews in conquered and allied countries raised problems for the diplomatic service. The systematic murder of five million persons is an enormous operation. It was successfully accomplished only because cooperation was so wholehearted and so general.

What does this say of the responsibility of the individual citizen? It is clear that no single person or small group could have made an effective protest. A priest, Dompropst Bernard Lichtenberg of St. Hedwig's Cathedral, in Berlin, openly asked prayers for the Jews. He was imprisoned for two years and then died on his way to Dachau. On the other hand, if there had been widespread national sympathy for the Jews and a reluctance to have them suffer, the work of extermination would have been rendered much more difficult. No such sentiment existed. What might have been the case if it had existed is shown by what happened in Italy. Although the Fascist government began to pass laws against the Jews in 1938 and was thus professedly anti-Semitic, these laws were applied without enthusiasm. Hitler met with all sorts of frustrations and received very little cooperation in his effort to exterminate the Italian Jews. While the individual may often prove helpless against totalitarian government, not even such a government can disregard massive public opinion.

It is appropriate to ask, finally, whether even those outside the German sphere of influence might not have shared some responsibility for the success of the anti-Jewish campaign. The question has recently been brought to the fore by the success of Rolf Hochhuth's play *Der Stellvertreter*, which accuses Pope Pius XII of unworthy motives in his failure to protest openly against the extermination of the Jews. The accusation is at least doubtful; for a vigorous public protest might have evoked such reprisals that it would have done more harm than good.[22] Somewhat harder to explain is the Allies' failure to bomb the extermination camps and the rail lines to them. By 1942 they had the needed information and a comfortable sufficiency of air power. Then, or even later, the lives of hundreds of thousands of Jews might have been saved.[23]

That an apparently refined and sensitive man like Ewald Peters should shoot down Jews in cold blood is not only shocking, it is perplexing. He, and others like him, do not seem to belong in any of the familiar categories of the criminal mind. There are criminals who frankly defy the moral law and the laws of the community, either habitually as a way of life or occasionally in a spirit of impulsive revolt. There are other criminals with clearly abnormal personalities, for example the psychopath with his conspicuous lack of self-control or the paranoiac with his delusions. These types, together with their subtypes and their combinations, are familiar; but Ewald Peters does not fit into any of them. Therefore, it is necessary to distinguish another type of malefactor, the citizen of a paramoral society who blindly follows that society's evil mores. Like the common criminal, he defies the moral law. Yet, unlike the common criminal, he does not revolt against society. He accepts it as it is, and so he gains respect as a reliable and responsible citizen.

This much is clear. Yet a mystery remains. How can a man who is both intelligent and sane, a man who regards himself and is regarded by others as decent and respectable, nevertheless commit acts of outright robbery and murder? How can he stifle his conscience? The question was discussed in a general way in the preceding chapter. Now it is appropriate to discuss it in the specific context of Nazi Germany.

The mechanism of repression supplies part of the answer. The destruction of the Jews was carried out in secrecy, as far as that was possible. Even among the killers themselves the subject was excluded from social conversation. When it had to be mentioned, euphemisms were used, such as the common one, "final solution of the Jewish question" (*Endlösung der Judenfrage*). This imposed silence prevented any public discussion of the moral issues, so that each individual had to face the problem alone. Much more widespread and much more effective, it seems, was the mechanism of rationalization. Probably anti-Semitic propaganda helped a bit here—the theory that Jews were "in control" and had to be eliminated. It is doubtful, however, whether this was taken very seriously except by a minority of fanatics. At least when the present writer was a student in Berlin and Frankfurt in 1931–32, the year before Hitler, it was not given credence by very many in student circles.

Most likely, the commonest and most effective rationalization was the theory of blind obedience: the citizen is not to examine the morality of official policy, his sole duty is to obey. From the standpoint of any ethic this is, of course, utter nonsense. However, for psychological insight into what happened in Germany, it is very helpful indeed. The principle, after all, has very wide acceptance. To realize this, one has only to remember how often Stephen Decatur's Norfolk toast, "Our country, right or wrong," is quoted with tacit approbation—even by churchmen. Whoever accepts this principle can scarcely criticize Ewald Peters who was, after all, merely carrying out official policy.

The doctrine of blind obedience seems to be a standard part of moral education throughout our Western civilization. It has been constantly reiterated: obey your parents; obey your pastor; obey your teacher; obey your foreman; obey the police. Very seldom is the point made that disobedience, too, can be a moral duty; yet, so long as this fact is forgotten, tyrants will rule their para-moral societies without too much difficulty.

Although the issue is controverted, one of the most striking proofs of the blind-obedience attitude in Hitler's Germany would seem to be the behavior of the Jews themselves. A large body of evidence appears to indicate that, on being ordered to do so, they cooperated actively in their own destruction. Such cooperation seems to have been very common. They would automatically assemble at a designated spot for deportation or shooting; and they would dig their own graves. It is not entirely surprising that Hitler's underlings should prove no less obedient than the victims themselves.

For those clearheaded enough to reject the doctrine of blind obedience, there were further confusing moral problems. First of all, there was the problem of cooperation. There could be no doubt that those who shot or gassed innocent Jews were guilty of a heinous deed; but how about those who cooperated at a distance and in seemingly minor ways? How about the government accountant who now and then had to handle Auschwitz items? How about the men responsible for the maintenance of the efficiency of the German railroads who realized that one function of these railroads was to convey Jews to their death? Remote cooperation of this sort was essential for the success of the complicated machinery of the extermination process. Yet, if an individual's cooperation appeared incidental and very distant, it could be easy to shrug off the problem.

For those with sensitive consciences who were worried about cooperation, there was a further question. Would justice be better served by a dramatic resignation from office, an act that might bring reprisals, or by staying on the job and using one's influence to ease somehow or slow down the destruction process? A striking example of the dilemma and a possible solution was furnished by Rabbi Leo Baeck, a leader of the German Jews, who approved the use of Jewish orderlies to pick up Jews for deportation on the ground that they would be more gentle than the Gestapo in handling the victims. A German functionary might easily take an analogous position on the ground that the fate of the Jews was inevitable, and that he might be in a position, as a government official, to ease the sufferings of the victims or perhaps even save some lives.

In the abstract, moral blame certainly attaches to anyone who cooperated in any way in the destruction of the German Jews. Yet it seems fair to admit that a great many of those who did cooperate remotely were not conscious of their guilt. As far as one can reconstruct it, the picture seems to be one of utter confusion of conscience. People were overwhelmed with moral problems which they were simply unprepared to meet;[24] and as they hesitated, tremendous social pressures were being applied. Under the circumstances, it took exceptional clearheadedness and heroic courage to decide to resist. It is not entirely remarkable that few did so.

This is perhaps the most disturbing fact which emerges from a study of the fate of the Jews under Hitler. The citizens of no country are trained to cope with the moral problems that arise in a paramoral society. They are trained on the assumption that the society in which they live is a normal one, that to obey the law and to obey conscience are one and the same thing. As long as the society in which they live actually is normal, this training is reasonably efficient. Most people do not grow up to become professional criminals. However, if there is a social cataclysm like Hitler's take-over, then conscience and mores point in different directions. For the common man, the result is complete confusion. In the case of Germany, a result of the confusion was five million murdered Jews.

4

The Bombing of Noncombatants

TODAY the savage immorality of the slaughter of the European Jews and the vicious evil of American Negro slavery are clear to everyone. Certainly, no civilized man would now dare to defend either slavery or genocide. Yet not everyone is equally clear about the immorality of the wartime bombing of noncombatants. We are still too close to the days of the Second World War. Too many of us were involved, directly or indirectly, personally or through relatives or friends. It is not altogether easy to gain proper perspective.

Let it be clear at the outset that we are not here discussing the morality of bombing purely military objectives, such as airfields, warships, army encampments, even though such bombing might have as an unintended side effect the killing of some noncombatants. What we are discussing here is the type of strategic act which is known as "area" or "obliteration" or "blanket" bombing. From what follows it should become clear that in this kind of bombing, noncombatant civilians are often directly attacked. This type of bombing, and this alone, is discussed in the present chapter; moreover, it is discussed only with reference to the Second World War. The enormously important question of a possible future atomic war will not be taken up.

The bombing of the Basque town of Guernica in the Spanish Civil War was not the first case of the bombing of civilian non-combatants; but it was this incident that first aroused the conscience of the world to the existence of a new and acute moral problem. On the afternoon of April 26, 1937, wave after wave of German planes bombed the town.[1] Inhabitants who fled were machine-gunned. Since Guernica was entirely undefended, the planes had sufficient time to do their job of destruction thoroughly. To the contemporary public such cruelty seemed incredible. The general reaction of the world was memorialized in Picasso's "Guernica," where the tortured victims writhe in agony.

During the Second World War, the technique of aerial warfare developed rapidly. Air power grew constantly in importance. New types of planes and bombs were developed along with new strategy and tactics. Part of this development involved the increased use of air power against noncombatants.

In the summer of 1940 the German bombing of England began; London and many provincial cities suffered. The bombing of Coventry seemed to contemporaries to symbolize particularly well the evil of obliteration bombing. This city was attacked in a number of air raids, the most severe being on the night of November 14–15, 1940. Many persons were killed and thousands were made homeless. Indignation was particularly acute over the almost complete destruction of the Cathedral of St. Michael, and it was, indeed, an irreparable loss. However, in judging the morality of such air attacks, the primary concern is the slaughter of human beings. A five-year-old child is infinitely more precious than a five-century-old church.[2]

The Allied air onslaught against Germany was somewhat slow

to develop. It was not until 1943 that a full-scale bomber offensive was launched. By that time, of course, American air power was deeply committed. In the discussions preliminary to the offensive two different procedures were considered. One was the precision daylight bombing of selected military and industrial targets, and the other was obliteration bombing at night of built-up industrial areas. In general, the Americans favored the former plan, whereas the British favored the latter. Gradually, the British view prevailed. The Casablanca Conference of January, 1943, played an important part in the decision.[3] From that time on, there seem to have been few scruples about the indiscriminate bombing of noncombatants.

Though the methods varied, the results were the same. Thus the British bombing of the Ruhr dams (Möhne, Eder, and Sorpe) on the night of May 16–17, 1943, released millions of tons of water which rushed through populated districts, drowning perhaps 1,200 civilians. During air raids, of course, a great many were killed either directly by the explosives or else by falling buildings. Gradually, however, the Allies realized that incendiary bombs could be even more effective, because when a great number of them were dropped on a city within a short time, so many fires were started that they became uncontrollable, and soon whole sections of the city were in flames. This became the preferred method of destroying built-up areas and their inhabitants.

The hideous effectiveness of fire bombing was illustrated particularly at Hamburg and Dresden. Between July 24 and August 3, 1943, the British made four night attacks on Hamburg, scattering incendiary bombs, and the Americans attacked three times by daylight during the same period. The result was a conflagration which destroyed three-quarters of the built-up sections of the city, killed more than 30,000 people, and made 900,000 homeless. Even more frightful was the destruction of Dresden in February, 1945. This was the war's most devastating attack on civilians. The destruction was so complete that the evidence is missing which would permit an exact accounting; but the most reliable estimates center around a figure close to 135,000 dead. The machinery of annihilation was becoming more and more effective.[4]

In the Far East, American techniques developed, as they did in Europe, from the precision bombing of industrial and military objectives to the wholesale bombing of cities. The most deadly instance of the latter was the bombing of Tokyo on the night of March 9–10, 1945. The target area was a rectangle of approximately three by four miles embracing "the heart of the congested residential district." The houses were so crowded together and so flimsily constructed that incendiary bombs soon kindled a great conflagration. Over a quarter million buildings were destroyed, nearly 84,000 persons were killed, 41,000 were wounded, and more than a million were rendered homeless.[5]

Of course, all previous air raids were completely overshadowed when nuclear bombs were dropped on Hiroshima and Nagasaki on August 6 and 9, 1945, respectively. These were not the most serious raids of the war in terms of human life: official estimates give 68,000 dead at Hiroshima and 38,000 at Nagasaki.[6] Many more had died at Dresden and Tokyo. Yet it was distinctive of the nuclear attack that a single bomb dropped from a single plane could have an effect comparable to that of wave upon wave of planes using conventional bombs. Each of the two bombs dropped on the cities had an energy yield of approximately 20 kilotons, that is, the effectiveness of 20,000 tons of TNT, the conventional explosive.

There were three causes of death at Hiroshima and Nagasaki—blast injuries, burns, and nuclear radiation. The first two were "conventional." Like the earlier explosive and incendiary bombs, the atom bombs killed by their mechanical and thermal effects, and they did this with incomparably greater efficiency than the earlier bombs. However, the most horrifying fact was that the atomic devices had introduced a completely new weapon, nuclear radiation, and the more that was learned about this new weapon, the more dangerous it appeared. Radiation could kill directly within hours or within weeks, while among survivors it could cause delayed injuries such as cataracts or leukemia. Children of irradiated parents might suffer adverse genetic effects, and long-term dangers from fallout could involve future generations. Nuclear weapons posed a manifold threat, and it soon became clear that they would be difficult to control.[7]

For estimating the effects of obliteration bombing, there are usually accurate figures about the destruction of property, for example the number of acres devastated or the number of buildings destroyed. In some instances, there are fairly good estimates of the number of human casualties. What is infinitely more difficult to grasp, however, is the effect as a human experience on those attacked. There are indeed descriptions like the following by a survivor at Hiroshima: "It was a horrible sight. . . . Hundreds of injured people who were trying to escape to the hills passed our house. The sight of them was almost unbearable. Their faces and hands were burnt and swollen; and great sheets of skin had peeled away from their tissues to hang down like rags on a scarecrow. They moved like a line of ants. All through the night, they went past our house, but this morning they had stopped. I found them lying on both sides of the road so thick that it was impossible to pass without stepping on them."[8]

Such accounts give some faint notion of the horror that reigned in the bombed cities. Yet what they describe is so remote from our range of experience that the imagination fails. We can understand events in which we ourselves have participated, and from these we can extrapolate for a certain distance. We can imaginatively combine bits of experience into new patterns and gain some idea of what it would be like to have participated in this or that event which we have never encountered personally. However, beyond a certain point the process breaks down. Those who have not been through it can never imagine what Hiroshima was like. Or Dresden. Or Hamburg.

Casualty figures may leave us unmoved because they refer to mass phenomena, whereas human tragedy is something individual. The mere statement that 30,000 died at Hamburg is too cold and statistical to give much insight into the suffering involved. It is only when we look through and beyond the figures that we may perhaps learn to sense in some degree the realities which the figures reflect. Then we begin to realize that these figures mean that these particular children, who will never again feel their mother's loving touch, died a slow and agonizing death. They mean that this promising young scientist will not live to fulfill his promise. They mean that this husband and father will return to an empty house. They mean that these once care-free teen-agers will go through life blinded or maimed and disfigured. Casualty figures mean all this and much more—unfortunately, only few men have the insight to experience such meaning.

Where relevant figures are available they reveal a high proportion of women among the victims. For example, in the Hamburg raids of July and August, 1943, the ratio of women to men killed was more than three to two.[9] Since one can presume that most active males were in the armed forces, it seems a fair guess that the men killed in the raids included mainly the aged and incapacitated. Figures also show that the number of children killed was considerable.

In post-war surveys of the effects of obliteration bombing, two facts revealed the erroneous judgments used by military leaders to rationalize the mass raids. One was that "German morale had not broken, as captured leaders proudly pointed out after the war."[10] This was equally true of the results of the German bombing of the British. The other fact was that "the direct effects of strategic bombing on the size of the labor force never grew to significant proportions" in Germany.[11] If those responsible for the bombing hoped that it would either break the spirit of civilians or interfere with production by creating a labor shortage, they must have been disappointed.

A writer discussing the bombing of Germany has rightly raised the following question: "Does the question of conscience arise at all for a man who releases a block-buster, unaimed, over a town filled with defenceless people? Does he wonder where it is going to explode? In a nursery, in an old people's home, in a hospital

75

ward?"[12] However, the moral problem is not one that affected the bombardier alone. It affected all the civil and military officials who established the policy of obliteration bombing and who helped to carry out that policy. Beyond them, it affected all the citizens of a democratic country who actively approved that policy or who passively consented to it by their silence.

One point must be kept clearly in mind when the morality of obliteration bombing is discussed. It is never permissible, under any conceivable circumstances, to do evil that good may follow from it as a result. The morality of obliteration bombing must be examined in itself. Of course, all this is elementary. Therefore, it is shocking that President Truman still justifies the bombing of Hiroshima and Nagasaki arguing that the attacks "ended the war" and "saved lives."[13] It is disturbing to reflect that a man who wielded such enormous power should have been so naïve about a moral issue.

What makes the situation all the more tragic is the fact that the bombing of Hiroshima and Nagasaki was so needless. Post-war surveys showed "how thoroughly the will to resist had been crushed by conventional weapons" used against Japan before the atom bombs.[14] It may be true that the American authorities did not realize this. In any case, it is quite likely that the atom bomb hastened surrender; but did the power of the bomb have to be demonstrated by slaying a hundred thousand civilians? A committee of scientists involved in the bomb project (the Committee on Social and Political Implications) proposed that the bomb should not be used as a weapon until its power had been demonstrated on a desert or a barren island in the presence of United Nations observers.[15] This would have been quite feasible. As another alternative, the bomb might have been dropped on Japan itself at some uninhabited location. The American authorities had already tried out the bomb for their own information at Alamogordo, New Mexico.[16] The test was completely convincing. The power of the bomb could have been demonstrated to the Japanese, too, without killing a hundred thousand human beings.

The morality of obliteration bombing, then, must be examined in itself. The principle involved is that no one may directly cause the death of an innocent person. Since the principle, as here applied, is so extremely important, let it be stated in the precise language of moral theologian John C. Ford, S.J. He writes: "I do not believe any Catholic theologian, in the face of conciliar and papal pronouncements, and the universal consensus of moralists for such a long time, would have the hardihood to state that innocent non-combatants can be put to death without violating natural law. I believe that there is unanimity in Catholic teaching on this point, and that even in the circumstances of a modern war every Catholic theologian would condemn as intrinsically immoral the direct killing of innocent non-combatants."[17]

This principle seems to be clear beyond debate. However, before it is applied to the concrete realities of the Second World War, two questions have to be answered: (1) Was the killing of the noncombatants "direct"? That is to say, was it the immediate purpose of the bombing or was it, on the other hand, an unintended and regretted side effect? (2) Could the civilians killed, or most of them, be rightly classified as noncombatants under the conditions of a modern total war?

Certainly, the death of civilians must never be intended di-

77

rectly as the immediate purpose of a bombing raid.[18] However, it is also an accepted principle that one may perform a good or indifferent act for a good purpose even though this act may indirectly, as an unwilled side effect, produce certain evil results. This is mere common sense; for it is unfortunate but true that the sincerest acts of virtue often have incidentally some regrettable consequences. As it applies to bombing, this principle means, for example, that one could legitimately bomb a railway bridge, even though some civilians who happened to be in the vicinity might be killed. Obviously, however, there must be a proportion between the benefit resulting from the attack and the incidental evil. The Lusitania was carrying guns and ammunition from the United States to the Allies; but that did not justify a German submarine in sinking the ship with a loss of 1,153 lives. Similarly, the argument that the direct purpose of obliteration bombing is the destruction of military objectives and that the killing of civilians is a mere unwilled side effect is clearly wrong. The facts speak for themselves; for it is entirely obvious that the direct and most important effect of the raids at Dresden or Tokyo or Hiroshima was the death of tens of thousands of civilians. It is indeed true that in these raids a number of installations of strategic importance were also destroyed; but it would be the height of absurdity to argue that the bombing was primarily an attack on these installations and that the civilian deaths were merely incidental.

It is clear that the deliberate killing of noncombatants by obliteration bombing is not morally justifiable; but the question remains whether the civilians bombed in the Second World War were actually noncombatants. Modern total war is so different from the wars of the past that the distinction between combatants and noncombatants is possibly blurred. But is it blurred to the point that civilians may be attacked like the men in uniform as unjust aggressors? First of all, it is beyond argument that *at least* part of the civilian population consists of noncombatants. This is true of young children, the chronically ill, inmates of mental hospitals, the lower grades of the feeble-minded, the senile, and others. At the opposite extreme there are civilians whose full-time jobs are directly connected with the prosecution of the war. The most salient examples are workers in munitions factories without whose product an armed force would be helpless. Then there are transport workers who move troops and keep them supplied. Again, there are civilian government workers who account for funds used for military purposes and maintain these funds by collecting taxes. It would not be hard to add other examples. Can such workers be treated as combatants in the same sense as soldiers in uniform? It is doubtful since even international law tends to limit combatant status to those who actually bear arms; but for the sake of argument let the question be here answered in the affirmative.[19]

There nevertheless remains a large class of civilian workers whose duties have no clear connection with the war effort. Random examples could be anything from milliners, piano tuners, and sextons, to cleaners and dyers.[20] It is obvious that these must be classed as noncombatants. This is not to assert that in the case of an unjust war such persons are entirely innocent; for they may aid the unjust war by their moral support, by buying war bonds, by attending to the needs of munitions workers, and in other ways. If their country is defeated, the victors may punish

79

such persons, for example by taxing them to raise funds for reparations. What is asserted here is that such persons, though not objectively innocent, are guilty of only indirect and remote cooperation, and that such cooperation is not a sufficient excuse for killing them.

There exists a principle called the *moderamen inculpatae tutelae,* which may be paraphrased "the limits imposed by a just defense." Defense must be strictly limited to that which is necessary to stop the aggression. Enemy soldiers actively prosecuting an unjust war may be killed when there is no alternative way to stop their aggression; however, the killing must be limited to combatants. To defend one's country it is not necessary to kill a piano tuner who bought one of his government's war bonds.

It is clear that the vast majority of civilians bombed during the war were noncombatants. A most careful study of this point was made by Father Ford, who deliberately adopted a very broad definition of "combatant," and who nevertheless found that even under this broad definition and even in typical industrial areas in wartime, at least two-thirds to three-fourths of the inhabitants would have to be classified as noncombatants.[21]

In the light of the foregoing considerations it seems clear beyond any doubt that the obliteration bombing of built-up residential areas, as practiced during the war, was a morally unjustifiable slaughter of human beings.[22]

The bombing of noncombatants in war is, therefore, one more example of a vast wrong for which decent and respectable citizens were responsible. The Allies made no secret of their bombing policy and the general public was well aware of what was going on. There were, indeed, scattered protests, from individuals, from the "historic peace churches," and from other small groups. However, there was never at any time a sufficiently large body of public opinion mobilized against the policy of obliteration bombing to force a reconsideration of it.

It is difficult to understand why there was so little effective protest. In the case of Catholics this silence was particularly appalling because Catholic moral doctrine has traditionally been applied not only to the conduct of individuals, but also to the policies of the organized community. Since the latter part of the last century the Catholic social movement and the great social encyclicals have given striking evidence of the Church's concern in social matters. Machinery had long existed in this country to translate this concern into practical action: specifically, the Catholic Association for International Peace was set up as a national organization to speak for American Catholics on matters of international relations.

By late 1944 the mounting extent of obliteration bombing was clear to all. The summer before, the destruction of Hamburg had given a horrible example of what was to come. In the meantime, Pius XII had again and again condemned the policy. Here there is space to cite only some examples of his statements. In 1940 he had said: "More than once, to our great distress, the laws which bind civilized people together have been violated; most lamentably, undefended cities, country towns and villages have been terrorized by bombing, destroyed by fire, and reduced to ruins; unarmed citizens, even the sick, helpless old people, and innocent children have been turned out of their homes, and often killed."[23] Again, in his 1942 Christmas Broadcast, he said: "Mankind owes that vow to the many thousands of noncombatants, women, children, sick and aged, from whom aerial warfare—whose horrors we have from the beginning frequently denounced—has, without discrimination or with inadequate precautions, taken life, goods, health, home, charitable refuge or house of prayer."[24]

Quite clearly, Rome had spoken. Obliteration bombing had been condemned, and theologians had added the weight of their more detailed arguments. In September, 1944, Father Ford had published his 49-page article in which he simply applied standard Catholic teaching on the rights of noncombatants and concluded that obliteration bombing was immoral. Other theologians discussed the problem with various nuances; but no one reached radically different conclusions.

If American Catholics had acted, even as late as the end of 1944, they might have had an influence on policy; for they form an influential minority in the United States. If they could not have forced a change of policy, at least they would have publicly repudiated obliteration bombing. Yet this did not happen. There was no statement from the hierarchy. There was no wave of protest from large Catholic national organizations. If there were isolated protests in the Catholic press here and there, it could not be said that the trend of editorial opinion was towards a repudiation of the bombing policy. So American Catholics stood by passively while tens of thousands died at Dresden and Tokyo and Hiroshima and Nagasaki.[25]

Why did American Catholics fail to translate their doctrine into action? It cannot be said that any attempt was made by the government to force them into conformity with threats as was the case in Germany.[26] To the credit of governmental officials it can be stated that a remarkable liberty of conscience prevailed in the country during the Second World War. The Selective Service acts made provision for conscientious objectors, and pacifist publications such as *The Catholic Worker* maintained their anti-war position without interference. The present writer can add some personal testimony of his own. During this period he was active in anti-war organizations, served on the board of the National Council for Prevention of War, and opposed the bombing policy on the platform and in writing.[27] Yet never once was the slightest hint forthcoming from ecclesiastical or academic superiors that such activities ought to be curbed.

If American Catholics failed to protest obliteration bombing, most of them probably rationalized their conduct on the principle of obedience to properly constituted authority. Since the understanding of this principle is of crucial importance in the present discussion, some space must be devoted to it.

First of all, it is clear that a citizen must respond to all the legitimate demands that his government makes. This means more than mechanically complying with the laws; it means active cooperation in good government. It ought to be equally clear that a citizen must refuse to obey a law when he is morally certain that the law is immoral. He must refuse to cooperate with immoral policies. Moreover, he must do whatever he can, particularly in a democratic country, to have the immoral laws repealed and the immoral policies corrected. This duty of disobedience to evil directives ought to be evident beyond the slightest doubt. If one cannot maintain this duty of disobedience, then it can be reasonably argued that all the defendants at Nuremberg were guiltless; for in committing their atrocities, they were simply carrying out policies set down by a duly constituted, though evil government. It seems incredible that large numbers of Americans during the Second World War could have quoted with approval the clearly immoral principle, "Our country, right or wrong."[28]

There remains a third possibility. A citizen may be honestly in doubt whether a governmental law or directive is moral or immoral, and therefore whether it is his duty to obey or disobey. Suppose that the doubt remains even after he has carefully studied all the available facts. In such circumstances, the citizen must arrive at practical moral certainty that he is not guilty of the direct killing of the innocent before he may, with a clear conscience, take immediate part in death-dealing measures. He may arrive at this practical certainty on the basis of the teaching of the hierarchy (if he is a Catholic) and of the opinions of learned and prudent men. The presumption in favor of a legitimately constituted government may also help him to arrive at this practical certainty. Furthermore a draftee, who is ordered to take part in warlike action by his government, would be more easily justified in having recourse to such indirect solution of his doubt than would a volunteer. But in every case the citizen must achieve practical moral certainty that his personal conduct is licit before he acts. It is not licit for one to make it a settled policy to follow government orders blindly without a consideration of their morality.

To return to the question of obliteration bombing—it seems quite apparent that the majority of American Catholics approved the government policy in this matter without the necessary reflection on the moral issues involved. In the light of the facts

84

which we have reviewed it is clear that a citizen could, say, in the fall of 1944 be morally certain that obliteration bombing, as it was being practiced by the Allies, constituted a direct attack on noncombatants and was therefore clearly immoral by accepted principles. It is hard to imagine how any intelligent and well-informed Catholic, and above all members of the hierarchy, could have serious doubts either about the facts themselves or about the applicable principles.[29]

It makes one wonder about the effectiveness for moral education of the vast edifice of American Catholicism when one reflects how passive American Catholics remained while their air force was slaughtering noncombatant civilians, men, women, and children, by the tens of thousands. Pope Paul VI was later to call the bombing of Hiroshima an "infernal massacre" and an "outrage against civilization."[30] That judgment would be equally appropriate for the slaughter of noncombatants elsewhere, at Hamburg, at Dresden, at Tokyo, for example. Yet there was little protest, certainly no effective protest, from American Catholics. On the contrary, Catholic military men participated fully in the bombing. The hierarchy had approved the war;[31] and this approval was not withdrawn or modified when the policy of obliteration bombing became public. It is apparent, then, that contemporary Catholic opinion solidly if unthinkingly approved the massacre of the innocent.

5

The Subproletariat

THE problem of poverty is by its very nature drab and uninteresting. It lacks the horrible drama of wars and persecutions. It is essentially unromantic and in this it contrasts sharply with the gracious plantation life of the Old South which was the setting in which slavery flourished. Indeed, it is this very quality of dullness and commonplaceness that makes it so easy to overlook the problem of indigence and its tragic effects; for it is easy to disregard that which is merely part of the familiar scene.

It is an ethical and sociological truism that a certain minimum of material resources is necessary for one's full development as a human being. Obviously, one cannot survive in reasonably good health without adequate food, clothing, shelter, and health care. Yet this is not enough. A modest financial competence is needed if mind and spirit are to reach full fruition. One needs an adequate education plus the leisure and resources to enter adequately into the spiritual, cultural, and social movements of the day. Man's spiritual nature by no means frees him from reliance on the material.

It may sometimes seem a bit self-contradictory that the Church condemns the overeager pursuit of wealth and praises detachment from material things, yet at the same time encourages large-scale efforts to alleviate poverty and demands adequate wages for the worker as a matter of social justice. But this is no empty paradox. The Church praises moderation, not destitution. The members of the Holy Family at Nazareth were not paupers, and St. Joseph was a skilled workman with his own modest business.[1] If it is true that avarice corrupts the soul, it is also true that destitution stifles it.

Poverty is a world-wide problem; but for our purposes we will discuss the subject only as it applies to contemporary United States.[2] However, since America is now enjoying an unprecedented affluence, it is worth bearing in mind that whatever suffering results from indigence in this much favored land must surely exist in vastly aggravated form in less fortunate areas.

It is an undeniable fact that many people in this country lack the amount of material goods needed for full personal development. However, it is very difficult to estimate the percentage of the population which is thus disadvantaged. Some light is thrown on the question by a government study of what was called "the interim city worker's family budget."[3] This was an attempt to estimate the cost of a "modest but adequate" level of living for a more or less typical urban American family consisting of an employed husband, a wife not employed outside the home, a son, and a daughter. The budget was intended to be such as to permit "adequate living, according to prevailing standards of what is needed for health, efficiency, the nurture of children, and for participation in social and community activities."

The items included in the budget mentioned were priced in

twenty large American cities at autumn, 1959, prices. Totals ranged from $5,370 in Houston to $6,567 in Chicago, with an average at $6,084. If this figure could be taken as representing a "modest but adequate" level of living for the average American family, then it would seem that more than half such families were below this level; for the median family income for the country in 1959 was $5,417. Between that year and 1964 this median rose about 21.3 per cent while the cost of living rose about 6.5 per cent.[4] These figures involve so many uncertainties that no very definite conclusion can be drawn. At most, it may be stated cautiously that probably not more than about half of all American families enjoy an income that can be roughly described as at least adequate for personal development. Of course, this statement says nothing about those persons who live alone or outside the family unit.

Among those who cannot attain a "modest but adequate" level of living, a certain proportion are in actual "poverty"—a term which is also not easy to define precisely. All agree that "poverty" implies a rather extreme degree of indigence such that health itself is threatened and that anything like a normal family life is very difficult to maintain. However, to translate this rather generalized notion into really concrete terms requires some highly technical statistical analysis. Probably the most successful attempt to date at such an analysis is represented by the "SSA Poverty Index" developed by the United States Social Security Administration. This index is very helpful to anyone who wants to realize what poverty means and how extensive it is in this country.

To live above the poverty level, one must first of all have an adequate diet. The cost of such a diet can be estimated as follows.

The National Research Council has set up standards of nutritional adequacy. The U.S. Department of Agriculture has translated these standards into actual food plans compatible with the eating habits of Americans. Different food plans were suggested for different income levels, among which the lowest was an "economy" plan for "temporary or emergency use when funds are low." By using this food plan it is possible to estimate the minimum cost of providing families of various age and sex compositions with the bare essentials of diet. Studies have shown that low-income families spend about a third of their income on food. Thus the total cost of clothing, shelter, health care, and the remaining essentials other than food amounts to about twice the cost of food itself. The SSA Poverty Index is based on this fact. Knowing the cost of an economy diet containing the minimum essentials, one may multiply this figure by three and thus estimate the total cost of maintenance at a corresponding minimum level. In this way, one obtains a cut-off point for poverty. Such cut-off points were calculated for families of various age and sex composition and also for individuals of various ages and both sexes not living with a family. Different figures were used for farm and nonfarm families because the former generally raise part of their food on their own land.

In March, 1965, the Current Population Survey gathered information about the 1964 income of Americans. Then special tabulations were made to determine how many persons, both family members and unrelated individuals, were living in poverty as defined by the SSA Poverty Index. It was found that out of a total noninstitutional population of 189.7 million, 34.1 million, or 18.0 per cent, were living in poverty.[5] It is interesting to note that several other estimates of the extent of poverty in the 1960's, although using quite different methods, tended to give rather similar results.[6] It seems, then, fairly safe to conclude that a fifth, or almost a fifth, of Americans now live in actual want, that they lack adequate food to maintain health, and that they are disadvantaged to a comparable degree in regard to housing, clothing, and other essentials.

We wish, however, to deal not with the poor in general, but with a particularly disadvantaged group of the poor which will be called the *subproletariat*. By this term will be designated all those who show the following characteristics: (1) They are members of families whose income is not more than two-thirds of the minimum defined by the SSA Poverty Index, or they are unrelated individuals whose income is deficient to that degree. (2) They are not regularly employed or they are members of families whose head is not regularly employed. (3) They are culturally isolated and feel themselves excluded from the main current of contemporary American life.

It is hard to estimate how many persons in this country should be classified as members of the subproletariat. It seems that more than half the poor have incomes no greater than two-thirds of the SSA cut-off minimums; thus they would constitute at least a tenth of the country's noninstitutional population.[7] It is more difficult to determine how many persons are "not regularly employed." At any given time in recent years about 95 per cent of the labor force has been classified as employed; but, of course, not all those employed at a particular time are regularly employed, and among the employed are many who work only part time.[8] It is important to remember also that any unemployed person who is not actively seeking employment is classified as "not in the labor force." Among these are an unknown number of persons who would like to work but who have given up the quest for work because they feel that there is no possibility of being hired.[9] Finally, it is obviously not feasible to try to estimate the number who would be included under the third criterion of the subproletariat, namely, cultural isolation. Although it is impossible to estimate the size of the subproletariat, it is certainly large enough to constitute a national scandal and tragedy.

In studying the subproletariat, it is essential to remember that it has not been defined exclusively by its economic characteristics. The subproletariat has a culture of its own, and this fact sets it apart. The word "culture" is here used in its richest anthropological sense to denote the sum total of immaterial things that can be handed down from generation to generation, beliefs, attitudes, values, etiquette, customs, techniques, symbols. Social groups have their distinctive cultures and a person reared in one culture may find it hard to adapt himself to an alien one. Because the subproletarian has his specific cultural traits, he does not fit easily into the standard American middle-class educational, economic, *or* social system.

Poverty without cultural isolation can be tolerable. The popular notion that great poetry has been written in the slums and that artists have painted masterpieces in garrets no doubt contains its share of truth. Such poets and painters presumably suffered the physical discomforts of the subproletariat, but they were buoyed up by the realization of their own talent and confidently looked forward to the day when they would be recognized. Indeed, many people can be poor without being miserable. A young physician serving his internship in a hospital may be very poor by the economist's dollars-and-cents criterion. Yet he is not a cultural isolate, he has a significant role to play, and his status is quite different from that of an uneducated man temporarily earning adequate wages as a construction worker, but without much hope of ever progressing very far beyond the status of common laborer. The two men may have comparable incomes at the moment, but their places in society are utterly different.

The cultural distinctiveness of subproletarians is very well illustrated by their language. This was the object of a study made in the Department of Sociology in the Catholic University of America.[10] The speech of seventy-four persons of very low social status living in an inhabited alley in Washington was studied. Rather sophisticated methods were used, including analysis of tape recordings by a sound spectrograph. The study demonstrated very clearly that these alley dwellers spoke a dialect quite distinct from Standard English in its phonetics and to a lesser degree in its grammar and vocabulary.[11]

Many persons believe that the speech of the lower socio-economic classes represents a bungling and unsuccessful attempt to speak Standard English in the sense that the high-school French of an American tourist in Paris represents an unsuccessful attempt to speak Standard French. This is not the case; the varieties of Substandard English are not imitations of anything. They are dialects in their own right and they are "substandard" only in the sense that they are unfashionable. To take a common example —the double negative is now considered "incorrect," though the construction was in good usage for many centuries as an emphatic negative and became unfashionable only in the eighteenth century. Therefore, when a subproletarian says, "I didn't do nothing," he is not making a mistake. He is simply speaking his own dialect which is different from Standard English, far less fashionable than Standard English, but certainly not inferior to Standard English by any abstract and objective criterion. What is here said about the double negative can be said of all the features of the pronunciation, grammar, and vocabulary of the various English dialects. In no aspect is the Substandard English spoken by the subproletarians a mere unsuccessful imitation of Standard English.[12]

The language of the subproletariat has been discussed here at what may seem to be disproportionate length in order to illustrate a point of essential significance. The culture of the subproletariat must be approached with an open mind. The middle-class investigator who starts with the assumption that his own dialect is "good" English and that the language of the subproletariat is "incorrect" or "corrupt" will never attain an objective viewpoint. What is true of language is true of other culture elements. They must be approached without preconceived value judgments. Bias is fatal to understanding, and it makes serious scientific work impossible.

Children from the subproletariat do not succeed very well in school. They tend to receive low grades and to drop out of school early. Thus there is an association between low income and lack of education. In 1964 the median income for families whose heads had completed less than eight grades of school was $3,462; for families of college graduates, it was $9,709. Although less than 11 per cent of families had incomes under $2,000 (the approximate cut-off point for the subproletariat), 27 per cent of the families whose head had less than an eighth-grade education belonged in that class.[13]

The lack of scholastic success among lower-class children used to be explained by their alleged low intelligence. It is indeed true that these children tend to have low I.Q.s as measured by standard tests. However, intelligence tests do not measure intelligence directly. They measure achievement; and only when opportunities are similar is achievement an index of comparative intelligence. For example, most tests are heavily weighted for verbal ability. If two children grow up in similar environments, then indeed the child who shows greater verbal ability is likely to appear the more intelligent. It is easy to understand, however, why such a test would not be fair when administered to a subproletarian child who speaks, as was pointed out above, a special dialect of English. Then there are other, more subtle, handicaps for the slum child. He may lack rapport with the tester and this makes him ill at ease. He may be less motivated to do well in an examination of the I.Q. type than upper-class children are. All in all, in the light of modern experience, it would seem rash to conclude that subproletarian children have less-than-average intelligence.[14]

It is sometimes alleged that slum children are poorly motivated because their parents do not appreciate the value of education and do not encourage them. It is probably not true that parents lack interest; but it may well be that, lacking a social bond with the school, they cannot make their interest effective, for example, by PTA activity.[15] Some believe that the child from the impoverished and overcrowded slum home lacks the pre-school experiences which should prepare him for formal education: there are few books and periodicals in his home to awaken a desire to learn to read; he lacks the playthings which help to develop manipulative skills; he is less likely than middle-class children to be taken on trips, even short trips around the city, which might broaden his intellectual horizon. Doubtless, such factors are handicaps, but it is difficult to assess their total importance.[16]

Recently, the opinion has been growing that the school itself bears the chief responsibility for the poor scholastic achievement of slum children. Teachers and administrators are likely to be from the middle class and the school system is likely to be permeated by middle-class values. This may result in outright discrimination. August B. Hollingshead found that influential citizens in "Elmtown" would exert subtle and not-so-subtle pressures for discriminatory treatment in favor of their children.[17] James B. Conant was shocked at the contrast between the fine schools of suburbia and the poor schools of the slums.[18] It is often the case that young and inexperienced teachers are sent to slum schools, while the older teachers use their seniority rights to obtain placement in more congenial neighborhoods.

School people sometimes discriminate against slum children without being consciously unfair. There exists what Frank Reissman calls "discrimination without prejudice."[19] Even sympathetic teachers may fail to understand the slum child and may grossly underestimate his abilities; then the children are quite likely to conform unconsciously to their teachers' low expectations. The resulting atmosphere is dreary and unstimulating, as teachers and pupils mechanically perform their given tasks. Under the circumstances it is not surprising that slum children often drop out of school as soon as they legally can.

Lately, in various places, school authorities have become aware of these facts and have launched special programs for underprivileged children, based on the simple assumption that these children are fully educable if only their teachers have faith in them and they have faith in themselves. The spirit of one such program, Higher Horizons in New York City, is thus described: "If we are to raise the educational, vocational, or aspirational levels of the child, we must first convince him that it is possible. A major effort must be made to raise his self-esteem as a necessary preliminary to improvement in motivation and in achievement. The teacher is the key figure in the total process. She herself must first believe in the child and in the program; she must be the first to catch the contagion of enthusiasm."[20]

Programs such as this are still in the experimental stage and it is far too early to evaluate them. However, they do indicate that at least the education of the slum child is no longer regarded as an insoluble problem.

By definition, the members of the subproletariat are irregularly employed and have very low incomes. Naturally, the two conditions go together. For the 9.6 million workers 18 years or older who were unemployed at least five weeks in 1961, average wage and salary income was about $1,900 and average total income from all sources was about $2,300. The difference between the two figures was accounted for chiefly by unemployment insurance and Social Security payments.[21]

Of course, the characteristic subproletarian lack of education, discussed above, is one valid reason for this irregular employment. Many years of education are required for the professions; and a great many nonprofessional occupations also have more or less demanding educational requirements. However, lack of schooling is not the only handicap of the slum dweller. His cultural apartness is also a bar. Actually, it does not require much formal academic training to be a salesperson in a department store or a teller in a bank. Yet a person from the slums, whose manners and whose very speech betray his low socio-economic status, would not be accepted in such positions. Mobilization for Youth, an agency operating in the Lower East Side slums of New York City, obtained the consent of a large department store to employ some teen-agers from its area. It turned out that the girls selected were terrified at the prospect of being salesgirls and dealing across the counter with middle-class customers; to do so would have been to enter a strange and confusing world. The girls were finally placed in the store in behind-the-scenes jobs where they would not meet the public. There is indeed a tremendous gap between the slums and the middle class; and it is the upper and middle classes that control the nation's economic life.

It is sometimes alleged that the unemployed lack jobs through their own fault. A national survey failed to confirm this. One of its findings was: "In general, they [the unemployed] cannot be regarded as personally responsible for their own difficulties, unwilling to accept suitable jobs, more or less voluntarily unemployed, and only casually interested in an occasional job."[22] Unemployment in the subproletariat is usually not a personal matter at all, but a built-in feature of subproletarian life. It is a handicap which only a very exceptional person can overcome.

Excessive illness and premature death are equally the lot of the subproletariat. The poor simply are sick oftener than the well-to-do. A recent study showed that persons with family incomes under $2,000 averaged 12.0 days of bed disability per year, whereas those with family incomes of $7,000 or more averaged only 5.2 days.[23] The same study found class differentials in the amount of chronic illness serious enough to limit activity. Of persons with family incomes under $2,000, there were 28.6 per cent suffering such limitations; the figure was only 7.9 per cent for those in the $7,000 or more family income class.[24]

Workers in the occupations characteristic of the lower classes have excessively high death rates. A good index of this is the standardized mortality ratio (SMR) which "compares the tabulated numbers of deaths in an occupation with the number to be expected had the death rate for the total male population with work experience prevailed in that occupation."[25] An SMR of 100 for a particular occupation would mean that the workers in that occupation had the same death rate as the whole population studied. The SMR applied to males aged 20 to 64 years showed quite striking differences between major occupational groups. For "professional, technical, and kindred workers" it was 88; for "managers, officials, and proprietors, except farm" it was 89; for "clerical and kindred workers" it was 84. In contrast, the SMR was 163 for "laborers except farm and mine."[26] The death rate for common laborers is thus almost twice as high as the rate for typical white-collar categories.

Indirect evidence for the association of high morbidity and mortality rates with social class is furnished by vital statistics for the country's nonwhite population. The existing high differentials cannot be explained by inherent racial differences; there is no reason to believe that Negroes are less resistant to disease than whites.[27] The only plausible explanation is that Negroes are on the average very much poorer and that they thus share the bad health characteristic of the poor. Existing differentials are large indeed. In 1962 the infant mortality rate was 22.3 per 1,000 for whites and 41.4 for nonwhites; maternal mortality rates were 23.8 and 95.9 respectively per 100,000 live births.[28] Expectation of life at birth was 67.6 and 74.4 for white males and white females; the figures were 61.5 and 66.8 for corresponding nonwhites.[29] In America's highly stratified society, being white confers the privilege of living six or eight years longer.

It is not hard to discover reasons for the prevalence of disease and death among the poor. Although, as we pointed out above, persons with family incomes under $2,000 have higher rates for bed disability and for chronic illness than persons with family incomes over $7,000, the former have fewer physician visits per year than the latter (4.6 as against 5.7) and a smaller percentage have hospital insurance (34.1 as against 87.5 per cent).[30] It is true that a great deal of free medical service is available to the poor in clinics; but there are practical difficulties in the system. If a person must take time away from his job to attend the clinic, with consequent loss of pay, then the service is not really free. If the clinic is at some distance, then the only feasible way for a person in weak health to get there may be to take a taxi which, again, is an expense. It sometimes happens that a clinic will give a free diagnosis, but the patient must buy the medicines prescribed. There are other ways, too, in which the prescribed treatment may be too expensive for the poor. The clinic physician orders a heart patient to curtail his physical activity. Even though he realizes that it is a matter of life and death, it may be very difficult for the patient to follow the doctor's orders if he knows no way to support himself and his family except physical toil.

The poor housing of the slums is deleterious to health. Acute respiratory disorders, skin diseases, and common infectious diseases of childhood spread more easily where there is poor heating, poor ventilation, crowded sleeping arrangements, and multiple use of water and toilet facilities. Various digestive disorders are related to the lack of proper facilities for the refrigeration of food. Crowding, poor lighting, and poor repair of living quarters increase the rate of home accidents.[31]

The SSA cut-off point for poverty was defined as a level where the income would permit a barely adequate economy diet. The income for the subproletariat is, by definition, no more than two-thirds of this. It is easy to guess that the diet at such a level must be very deficient. A study of the diet of persons living in the inhabited alleys of Washington, D.C., showed that they were forced to use foods of high satiety value, but low in vitamins. Choice of food was so limited that a balanced diet was impossible. Moreover, meals were irregular. Interestingly enough, the alley dwellers used a considerable quantity of edible wild plants such as dandelions or pokeweed, which they gathered in vacant lots or along the river bank, to supplement their regular diets.[32]

In the United States we do not put the poor to death in gas chambers like the Jews at Auschwitz. We shorten their lives in less dramatic ways, by forcing them into unhealthy slums with inadequate diets and without proper health care.

But it is a mistake to imagine that the greatest hardship of the subproletariat is the endurance of the physical conditions of life in the slums, the inadequate diet, the overcrowding, the paucity of constructive recreational facilities, the sickness, the high death rates. The essential tragedy of the slums is the constriction of opportunities for full development of the personality. To be fully human, one's spiritual and mental capacities must attain a certain fruition. The life that falls short of this goal is, to that extent, a failure. In the slums, this human failure is usually overwhelming, withering, disastrous.

Slum dwellers desperately need understanding; but unfortunately they are apt not to receive it. The same social gap which makes it difficult for a subproletarian child to adapt himself to the middle-class school and, later, to the economic world also makes it hard for the middle class to understand the subproletariat. The two cultures reason from different premises and therefore they interpret the same facts differently. Besides, when white-collar people such as school teachers or employers deal with slum dwellers, they deal with them in formalized situations which lack the spontaneity and freedom of intra-class companionship. There is little real dialogue between the classes.[33]

101

In the subproletariat teen-agers must soon become self-supporting. The nature of the difficulties they encounter when they enter the economic world has already been touched on. In practice these difficulties mean that the teen-age dropout finds it very hard to obtain any sort of employment at all. If he can find employment, it is almost sure to be in some low-paid, monotonous, blind-alley job.[34] Similarly, where most people find a deep emotional satisfaction in marriage and family life, there are almost insuperable obstacles to such satisfaction in the slums. By definition, the subproletarian level of living is inadequate for the bare necessities. This not only undermines health, but also produces harmful psychological stresses. Personality clashes are intensified by overcrowding. Because of lack of room in the home, children must spend much of their play time on the streets away from parental supervision. It does not take much imagination to realize that, for these and similar reasons, a normal, relaxed, emotionally satisfying family life is difficult to attain in the slums.

Although all subproletarian family life is greatly constricted by intense poverty, aside from this one fact it is very hard to make generalizations. All the problems of upper-class family life have their parallels in the slums. One rather surprising finding is that love, loyalty, and deep affection can exist between husband and wife and between parents and children even amidst the strains of unspeakable poverty. Of course, child-rearing is grossly defective under such circumstances. Family life cannot, by any stretch of meaning, be called normal. However, the abnormality in these families is due entirely to their impoverished condition. The right interpersonal attitudes are present and they could be the basis of a pleasant and normal family life, were it not for the grinding poverty.[35]

It would be vastly illuminating for a middle-class person if he could see the world through the eyes of the subproletarian. He would see a world without much hope, a world of narrow intellectual horizons, a world of physical suffering and disease, a world where normal interhuman relationships are difficult, a world which even the consolations of religion penetrate with difficulty. No wonder that the young are angry in the slums and the old are without hope.

Slum areas are characterized by high crime and delinquency rates. To be interpreted fairly, however, this fact too, must be viewed in its proper perspective. Even in high-delinquency neighborhoods, actual delinquents are a tiny minority. In New York City in the two highest delinquency areas, Central and East Harlem, only about 3 per cent of the youth 6 to 20 years of age were actually arrested in the course of a given year.[36] On the other hand, it seems certain that children from the respectable classes commit a great many delinquent acts for which they are not apprehended.[37] There is also evidence that there is vastly more crime committed by the white-collar class than one would suspect from reading the police reports.[38] Crime and delinquency statistics are notoriously unreliable and it is impossible to make any realistic quantitative statements about the relative prevalence of lawbreaking in the various social classes. It is, however, rather obvious that crime is much more visible in the slums.

It is safe to assert, at any rate, that there are qualitative differences between the law violations of slum dwellers and those of white-collar people. The former are not likely to be guilty of restraint of trade or of misrepresentation in advertising, nor are

103

the latter likely to be involved in the fights of street gangs. The police are often not highly respected by the subproletariat. They may be viewed as the agency by which the middle class imposes its own mores on the slums. If the schools are oriented towards middle-class values and if the slum child finds little profit or satisfaction in them, he is nevertheless punished as a truant if he stays away. Slum dwellers often believe that the police are unduly harsh with them. For parallel reasons a term in jail is apt to be considered a less serious disgrace in the subproletariat than elsewhere. There is reason to suspect that occasionally crimes of violence against white-collar people are an irrational, possibly unconscious, protest against a class system that galls the subproletariat.

Like slavery, genocide, and obliteration bombing, the misery of the subproletariat is an enormous social evil that inheres in a social system controlled by decent and respectable people. It is indeed a cause for intense shame that in this country, in this day of unparalleled affluence, so many persons should be forced to live the scarcely human existence which we have described.[39]

There is one striking difference between the injustice suffered by the subproletariat and the injustices involved in genocide, slavery, and obliteration bombing. In the case of the subproletariat, it is very hard to pinpoint the responsibility. No one person and no group of persons deliberately planned the slums in the sense that Belsen was deliberately planned. The present socio-economic structure of our society is the end product of a long interplay of historical forces that are only imperfectly understood. However, if the upper and middle classes cannot be blamed for deliberately causing the miseries of the subproletariat, they can at least be blamed for their passivity in the presence of them.

Nevertheless, the upper and middle classes are not entirely indifferent to the plight of the poor in general. They have contributed generously to philanthropic causes. They have not opposed the trend towards social security and welfare legislation, or at least they have not opposed it actively enough to prevent the growing trend towards legislation of this sort. However, the interest of white-collar people in the poor tends to be discriminatory. They show sympathy towards those who used to be called "the worthy poor," that is, members of the reliable working class who have been impoverished by some misfortune beyond their control. The attitude towards the subproletariat is, on the contrary, quite unsympathetic. Thus in "Elmtown" members of the lowest class were thought to lack self-respect, to enjoy their dirty environment, to have no interest in health and medical care, to be too lazy to work, and to "have a criminal record for a pedigree."[40] What is shocking about such opinions is the implication that subproletarians do not have quite the same fundamental needs and aspirations as other human beings.

Since such attitudes exist, it is not surprising to find discrimination against the subproletariat sometimes in the form of outright exploitation, as for example, of migratory farm workers, of sharecroppers, or of other unorganized labor. What is probably more important, however, is the discrimination written into our social legislation. Such legislation is admirable in itself, and has helped to reduce poverty in the steady working class. It has, however, been of much less help to the subproletariat.

That social legislation tends to by-pass the slums is evident, for example, in the fact that many forms of social insurance are of little help to the subproletariat. All states have workmen's compensation laws providing both medical and cash benefits to workers injured on the job. There is a federal-state system of unemployment insurance to tide workers over periods of unemployment. The most comprehensive system of all is the federal Old Age, Survivors, and Disability Insurance (OASDI) which grants payments to retired workers, disabled workers, and certain survivors of deceased workers. There are also a number of pension plans or health and welfare plans set up by private industry. The reason why all these excellent programs do so little for the subproletariat is that they are all tied to employment in some way, and employment is very irregular in the subproletariat. Workmen's compensation obviously applies only to persons actually at work. Unemployment-insurance laws vary from state to state; but to qualify, the applicant must have a work record demonstrating a recent and substantial attachment to the labor force. A great many occupations are excluded by law. Among all systems of social insurance, OASDI is the most impressive and it is constantly being improved. However, even under this program benefits are related to the insured worker's earning record. Therefore, casual workers and all other workers whose annual earnings are very low receive relatively little help from the system. It becomes apparent, then, that the basic purpose of all social insurance plans, whether public or private, is to protect the stable working class against the hazards of their condition.

In addition to the various forms of social insurance, there are a number of federal, state, local, and private assistance programs designed to help various classes of persons who are demonstrably in need. These programs differ in principle from social insurance. They apply after a need has arisen, whereas social insurance aims to prevent the occurrence of the need. Assistance programs are actually a form of almsgiving, whereas recipients of social insurance benefits receive them as a matter of right and the question of need is not relevant. These assistance programs are particularly important for the subproletariat. The most important assistance programs are operated on a federal-state cooperative basis. These include old-age assistance (OAA), medical assistance to the aged (MAA), aid to the blind (AB), aid to the permanently and totally disabled (APTD), and aid to families with dependent children (AFDC). These are large programs. In 1964 more than two million persons were receiving OAA at a cost of over two billion dollars; and there were more than four and a quarter million persons in AFDC families receiving a total of over one and a half billion. Other programs were smaller than these, but nevertheless large in absolute numbers.

Large as they are, these assistance programs are far from meeting the needs of the subproletariat. The subject is complicated and here there will be space for some remarks about AFDC only. The obvious defect in this program is the failure to give families enough assistance to maintain themselves on a level of health and decency. In 1961 "the total income of AFDC families averaged $1,680, little more than half the $3,000 figure used as the poverty demarcation line in the President's estimate."[41] The situation is far worse in particular localities than the foregoing general statement indicates. AFDC is a federal-state program in which the individual states set eligibility standards and decide the amount of assistance which families are to receive. Often the amounts are very low. For example, in the case of a family consisting of a mother and three children, the highest monthly amount payable for basic needs is only $50.00 in Mississippi, $67.26 in Alabama, and $72.00 in South Carolina.[42] It is unnecessary to stress the point that these amounts are grossly inadequate.

A special problem exists in families where there is present an unemployed parent. Obviously, if a father is out of work and unable to find work, his wife and children may be in just as desperate need as though he were dead, disabled, or had left home. AFDC legislation did not provide for this type of family until 1961 when the states were given the option of extending assistance to it. However, at the present writing only eighteen states have taken advantage of the opportunity.[43] When close to 4 per cent of the labor force is unemployed, it is obvious that, even with the best will in the world, some persons must lose out in the competition for jobs. It seems cruel to penalize their families as a result. Under such circumstances it is not unusual for men to desert their families so that their wives and children may become eligible for AFDC.

The types of assistance that have been discussed are limited by law to certain defined classes of needy persons. However, there are many needy individuals and families who are not eligible under any of these programs. For them, the only recourse is what is called "general assistance," that is, relief not limited by specific requirements, but available on the basis of need alone. There is no federal program for this kind of aid. In different jurisdictions responsibility for it is assumed by the state, by the local unit of government, or by both cooperatively. Of course, there are also private philanthropic agencies whose relief policies are not lim-

108

ited by law, but their resources are comparatively modest. All in all, the general assistance picture is far from satisfactory, and there is an undeniable need of a national policy.

The success of welfare programs must depend in large measure on the quality of the personnel employed in them. In 1960 there were 105,000 persons in social welfare positions of whom "only about one-fifth . . . have the basic professional education that would qualify them as professional social workers."[44] There is reason to fear that the majority of untrained welfare workers do not have an altogether intelligent and sympathetic insight into the problems of the subproletariat.[45] Indeed, it is not altogether certain that even professional social workers have in all cases succeeded in overcoming their middle-class prejudices.

Recently, there have been some promising efforts to cope with the problems of the subproletariat. President Johnson's "war on poverty" involves a recognition of the complexity of the problem and of the need for attacking it on various fronts. It is necessary to raise the general level of prosperity of the country and reduce unemployment. Education must be improved and broadened. The disabilities which handicap the nonwhite population must be removed. Good health services must be made available to the very poor. Retraining is in order for workers displaced from their jobs. Certain disadvantaged areas of the country need special programs tailored to their special needs. It is refreshing to see that the policy of the Johnson Administration is not committed to a single panacea, but recognizes the complexity of the problems of the subproletariat by the versatility of the measures proposed.

The freshness of the new approach is illustrated by a provision in the recently approved legislation for health insurance for the aged ("Medicare"). The new law provides for hospital insurance and medical insurance. The premiums for hospital insurance are to be paid by employed persons and their employers. So far this is merely another example of social insurance like other programs of social security. However, the new law also provides that premiums shall be paid directly out of government funds for those outside the social security system. Thus the benefits of social insurance are extended to persons, such as the subproletarians, of whom few would otherwise be eligible.

This progress is encouraging; yet the problems of the subproletariat remain formidable. Too often the attitude of the white-collar classes is cold and unsympathetic. An unpleasant example of this has been presented by public expressions of opinion after the riots in the Watts section of Los Angeles. Criticism of the rioters for their lawlessness was universal. However, it was much less widely realized that the white citizens of the city must bear some of the blame; for the Negro was infuriated at their indifference to his plight. Both civic and religious leaders seemed generally unsympathetic. In the 1964 election the voters of the state had repealed a fair-housing law by a 2-to-1 margin in a referendum. Anti-poverty funds budgeted for Los Angeles had remained for the most part unused. Under the circumstances, the outburst of violence, if it cannot be pardoned, can at least be understood.

The self-righteousness of the dominant classes is sometimes a scandal. It is a crime to throw a brick through a store window and make off with a bottle of whiskey. Anyone caught by the police in such an act will be arrested, brought to the station house, perhaps treated harshly because of his race, and eventually punished with a severity not commensurate with his actual crime. Public opinion despises the looter. He is evil, antisocial, a misfit in society. But no guilt is incurred by the satisfied people with security, comfort, and prestige who vote against fair-housing laws, remain indifferent to civil rights, and refuse to be worried about the plight of the subproletariat. Yet by the standards of abstract justice they are perhaps also criminals. Are they not guilty in their indifference to their neighbors' suffering? It is to them that are addressed the dreadful words, "Inasmuch as you did not do it to one of these least ones, neither did you do it to me."[46]

111

6

Respectability Is Not Enough

THE preceding chapters have summarized "case studies" of a highly disturbing phenomenon. Vast and cruel injustice can exist with the active cooperation, or at least with the passive acquiescence, of decent citizens. How this can be is hard to determine precisely. It is difficult enough for the criminologist to understand why common criminals revolt against the moral and civil law. It is much more difficult to understand why respectable citizens aid and abet monstrous social crimes.

In our first chapter we attempted to give some reasons. The community insists on certain customary types of action—the mores. Citizens are coerced to follow these mores by various sanctions, ranging from social disapproval to the death penalty. In a paramoral society certain of the mores are contrary to the moral law, so that the citizen who realizes this fact must either act against his conscience or suffer certain unpleasant consequences; or he may, as a third alternative, stifle his conscience and act immorally. In any case, what usually happens in a paramoral society is that the citizens as a whole, including the decent and the respectable, will accept the mores, whether they are right or wrong.

This explanation is doubtless valid as far as it goes, but it leaves unanswered a more fundamental question. Why do the mores, with their attached sanctions, exist in the first place? Why does the organized community set up these standards of conduct, formal or informal, and why is there such great social pressure that they be observed? Why do the mores have so much prestige that in a paramoral society they take precedence even over the moral law itself?

The answer is not far to seek. The mores are essentially important because the social order could not be maintained without them. There could not be an organized community unless its members had agreed to follow certain standards, unless, for example, they had agreed to drive on the right-hand side of the road, to pay their just debts, to send their children to school, and to obey a thousand other rules and customs. Some of these are obviously arbitrary; we could, for instance, agree to drive on the left instead of the right. Some are based on the moral law; one must, in justice, pay one's debts. However, the essential fact is that all citizens must accept these standards, at least the principal ones and at least most of the time. Unless they did so, there could be no society; there could be only chaos, until a new set of mores was developed.

Loyalty to the mores, then, is simply loyalty to one's community. He who follows them strengthens existing society and earns the respect of his fellow citizens. He is respectable. In a moral society there is no conflict between morals and mores; one can be respectable and virtuous at the same time. However, in a paramoral society there are vast areas of conflict, and citizens are faced again and again with an unavoidable choice between the mores and the dictates of conscience. It is a choice between two ways of life. If a man decides to disregard his conscience and follow the mores habitually, whether right or wrong, he is actually following a perverted, though real, system of ethics which we have here been calling the ethic of respectability. This is a code of conduct as well as a philosophy of life. However, indefensible as it may be in the light of reason or religious teaching, the ethic of respectability does nevertheless provide a definite guide to behavior.

But a man who lives by the ethic of respectability cannot be said to be moral. His deepest motive of conduct is not the moral law or any religious principle. His ultimate loyalty is directed towards society-as-it-is. He lives to stabilize this society and thus gain the applause of like-minded men. He may appear virtuous because he is a very regular church member, pays his debts promptly, and is faithful to his wife. Really, however, he acts in this manner because it is regarded as respectable. The man is actually quite amoral.

It is not surprising that those most loyal to the established order are likely to be those who profit most from it. It is they, too, who are likely to follow the ethic of respectability most meticulously. Thus the most esteemed citizens will be those who control money, political power, and prestige, those men and their followers who profit by being connected with them. On the other hand, citizens with only a small stake in the established order have less reason to be loyal to it. The poor, the unemployed, members of minority groups, have small reason to feel constrained by the ethic of respectability.

The respectable members of the dominant classes go to great lengths to force their fellow citizens to observe the ethic of respectability. This is understandable. To attack the ethic of respectability is to attack the established order, and to do that is to attack the privileges of the privileged.

A striking example of the social significance of the mores and of the ethic of respectability which supports the mores is furnished by the slaveholding society of the Old South. The whole economic system of the region rested on the plantation with its slave labor. The gracious and charming life of the upper class was possible because obsequious slaves were available as house servants. Fundamental to the class system was the rule that every white person was accounted socially superior to every colored person; the poorest of the poor whites could bolster his ego with this thought. Not only the southern apologists for slavery, but even northern moderates, believed that the abolition of slavery would bring complete chaos, complete anarchy, to an entire region.

The bitter injustice of American Negro slavery was as obvious as any evil in history. Yet this clear fact could not be admitted, and fierce measures were used to suppress it. For example, a Louisiana law prescribed the death penalty for using "language in any public discourse, from the bar, the bench, the stage, the pulpit, or in any place whatsoever," that might cause "insubordination among the slaves."[1] Literally interpreted this would mean that a clergyman who denounced the immorality of slavery could be dragged from his pulpit and hanged. The punishment was threatened on no abstract ground of ethics. It was threatened simply and solely because the denunciation of slavery would undermine the region's socio-economic system.

The imposition of false moral standards by force is, of course, not at all uncommon. On the contrary, it is a regular feature of paramoral societies. Anyone in Cuba who should dare to denounce the evils of Castroism would not for long have his freedom. The persecution of the Jews was commendable by the ethic of respectability prevalent in Nazi Germany; to brand the persecution as immoral was to court disaster. A grim proof of this was the fate of Dompropst Lichtenberg who, after daring to pray openly for Jews in the Berlin Cathedral, was sent to prison for two years, and then died on his way to a concentration camp. Hitler was equally successful in coercing citizens to fight in his obviously unjust wars. After exhaustive investigation, Gordon Zahn could find among Catholics only seven who openly refused military service; of these, six were executed.[2]

There are methods more subtle than crude persecution to coerce public opinion into accepting the evil mores of a paramoral society. One is to obtain the approval, at least the tacit approval, of organized religion. To do this requires a certain moral dexterity, but it is far from being impossible.

In a normal, moral society, the cooperation of church and state is a natural requisite of the peace and well-being of the people. The state has the high function of "guiding its members to their greatest perfection in the material and temporal order."[3] Ideally, therefore, church and state should work together not only for such immediate goals as the preservation of public order with the suppression of theft and violence, but also for more comprehensive goals, such as the establishment of a socio-economic structure which conduces to the welfare of all citizens. It is thus understandable that statesmen and religious leaders should develop strong mutual respect and should become accustomed to cooperate readily in the pursuit of their common objectives.

But this condition can be disturbed if paramoral elements are introduced into government programs. Often this will take place, not openly, but silently and deceptively, so that religious leaders may find themselves facing a moral aberration which is an accomplished fact. They then must decide when and with what emphasis they should repudiate the state's unjustifiable policies. The whole situation can be complicated, as it was in Nazi Germany, by false propaganda, counter-accusations, and a generally intensified emotional atmosphere.

When Hitler came to power, he seemed to do so legally enough and there appeared to be no reason for the German citizens to refuse him the obedience due to a lawfully constituted authority. Pius XI concluded a concordat with the Third Reich which Hitler covertly began to violate almost immediately. He soon started to persecute the Jews, to develop a quasi-religious cult of the state, and to introduce other immoral policies. However, when the Second World War began, Hitler could as chief of the government demand the loyalty of all citizens in the defense of their fatherland. In this new situation, which engendered agonizing problems of conscience, there seemed to be little that the individual citizen could do.[4] Although he might protest openly he would as a consequence be shot or sent to a concentration camp, so that such a protest seemed futile. If he conspired to thwart

117

Hitler's war aims he would be tormented by the thought that he was betraying his country. The usual result was inaction, both on the part of Catholics and of members of other religious groups. There was little sustained and effective protest. Thus, much against their wills, religious leaders were placed in the embarrassing position of seeming to give a certain tacit approval to Hitler's paramoral society.

It must be admitted, of course, that religious leaders are not always merely trapped by circumstances. History knows only too many instances of spiritual leaders who were too cowardly to protest against an evil government or who voluntarily cooperated with it for their own selfish ends. The public profession of religious principles does not automatically make one virtuous. The Pharisees were not the only prominent churchmen who set themselves up as models of devotion and yet "left undone the weightier matters of the Law, right judgment and mercy and faithfulness."[5]

A paramoral society can obscure its perverse policies in an atmosphere of respectability by manipulating the machinery of law making and law enforcement. The law has naturally a certain majesty, since it exists for the application to specific situations of the abstract principles of right and wrong. And the law makes such application very theatrically. Anyone who has ever been present while sentence was being pronounced in a criminal court will realize this. The defendant stands manacled between guards; the judge sits at a raised desk, wearing robes which symbolize the impersonality of his office; the courtroom is hushed as the sentence is pronounced. It is a dramatic repudiation of the evil-doer by organized society, and a concrete manifestation of the public conscience. The distinction between right and wrong is presumably spelled out with the utmost clarity.

In a paramoral society, when evil laws are enforced by the courts it is very hard for the spectator to realize that the above situation has been completely reversed. The manacled defendant represents justice and the judge in his robes represents evil. Certainly, under the Third Reich it must have required an unusual clarity of thought and an unusual independence of judgment to grasp the fact that the prisoner at the bar might be standing there simply because he was courageous enough to resist the outrageous anti-Semitism of the state. It must have been hard for the average citizen to realize that the elaborate machinery normally associated with the maintenance of justice was being used to support the most infamous injustices. For even when the law is evil, it remains majestic; and its majesty remains impressive.

After the war, the major leaders of the Third Reich were put on trial for waging aggressive war and for "crimes against humanity." It is surely a laudable principle that those responsible for the conduct of a war should be held accountable for their actions; however, it is more than regrettable that in this instance the defendants should have been chosen exclusively from among the vanquished, and the judges exclusively from among the victors. For representatives of the Allies to have acted as judges would seem to have been a violation of the elementary principle that a judge should not be involved, either personally or as a member of some corporate entity, in the issues to be tried before him. It was particularly ironic that representatives of the cruel and despotic government of Stalinist Russia should have been selected to judge the "crimes against humanity" committed by others.

One thing the war-crimes trials achieved brilliantly: they dramatized the respectability of the Allies. That was perhaps their chief, though unadmitted—perhaps even unconscious— purpose. Possibly the British and American members of the tribunals may have felt an occasional scruple as they picked their way through the rubble of German cities where their bombers had so relentlessly slaughtered tens of thousands of noncombatants; but once in the courtroom their equanimity was doubtless restored. They cloaked themselves in the majesty of the law. Day after day, week after week, the evil deeds of the Germans were discussed in detail while the representatives of the Allies passed judgment on their enemies. It was not enough to win the war; the moral superiority of the victors had to be demonstrated.[6]

Respectability consists in conformity to the mores. The existence of a set of mores presupposes the existence of a society which imposes those mores and supports those who conform to them. As long as the Third Reich prospered, prominent Nazi officials enjoyed great prestige. With the aid of swarms of subordinates, they implemented public policy, they received honors, they lived in comfort, even during the widespread poverty of the period. By Third Reich standards, they were eminently respectable patriots. When the Third Reich vanished, their respectability vanished with it. During the war-crimes trials they stood at the bar in the shabby clothing of common criminals. Stripped of the insignia of

120

respectability, they could be seen for what they really were, dishonorable, immoral, craven men.

But during the trials it was impossible to overlook entirely certain parallels between the wartime conduct of the victors and of the vanquished. An interesting incident took place when the so-called "Einsatzgruppen Case" was being heard before a Nuremberg Military Tribunal. Technically, this was an international court because it had been set up under the authority of a four-power charter; but the arrangements were entirely in American hands and the personnel of the court was American. The twenty-three defendants had been associated with the mobile killing units which followed the German armies in their invasion of the U.S.S.R. in the summer of 1941 and which, as we have remarked, were responsible for the death of some 1,400,000 Jews. The trial has been rightly called the greatest murder trial in history.

The most important defendant was the Gruppenfuehrer (Major General) Otto Ohlendorf, an intellectual with a doctorate in jurisprudence and a former research director in the Institute for World Economy and Maritime Transport at Kiel. He had early joined the Nazi party and during the war he was put in charge of Einsatzgruppe D, a mobile unit which, by his own admission, had killed 90,000 Polish Jews. He was found guilty by the court and was executed in 1951.

During cross-examination Ohlendorf was asked whether it was the policy to kill Jewish children as well as adults. He replied that such was indeed the policy, although he personally had never seen children put to death. Then he added, in reference to obliteration bombing as practiced by the Allies, "I cannot imagine that those planes which systematically covered a city that was a fortified city, square meter for square meter, with incendiaries and explosive bombs and again with phosphorus bombs, and this done from block to block, and then as I have seen it in Dresden likewise the squares where the civilian population had fled to—that these men could possibly hope not to kill any civilian population, and no children. And when you then read the announcements of the Allied leaders on this—and we are quite willing to submit them as document—you will read that these killings were accepted quite knowingly because one believed that only through this terror, as it was described, the people could be demoralized and under such blows the military power of the Germans would then also break down." [7]

The Einsatzgruppe commanded by Ohlendorf followed the invading armies of the Third Reich into enemy territory, rounded up Jews, and slaughtered them. The planes of the U.S. Army Air Forces slaughtered the civilian inhabitants of enemy cities by bombing. In both cases the victims belonged in the same category; in both cases they were noncombatant enemy civilians, men, women, and children. The Einsatzgruppen killed those who happened to be Jews; the Army Air Forces killed those who happened to be in a certain city at a certain date. Apart from the overwhelming perverseness of genocide as such, from the moral standpoint the instances offer a number of tragic parallels. The moral responsibility of the participants was quite comparable in the two cases. As the Nuremberg Military Tribunal correctly pointed out, the duty of obedience does not excuse a subordinate who carries out the immoral orders of his superior.[8] There is no question that Ohlendorf should have refused to slaughter the Polish Jews, just as the American airmen should have refused to slaughter the civilian inhabitants of cities. However, it is more than naïve to expect military men in the heat of warfare to display a greater moral sensitivity than leaders of public opinion at home who can examine the morality of national policy in a less emotional atmosphere.

Certainly, the crew of the B-59 which set out from Tinian early in the morning of August 6, 1945, to bomb Hiroshima and the crews of the observation planes which accompanied it were not encouraged to question the morality of their act. In fact, before taking off, they attended "religious services."[9] Then, having implored God's blessing, they rose from their knees, these pious young men, and proceeded to perpetrate what Pope Paul VI was later to call "an infernal massacre." One may wonder whether the bomb crews felt any scruples during their long trip back to Tinian. Did they think of the tens of thousands they had slaughtered? Of the sufferings of the survivors? If they did, reassurance awaited them. As the crews alighted, General Carl A. Spaatz greeted them, presenting the commanding officer with the Distinguished Service Cross and the others in the crew with appropriate medals.[10]

From the standpoint of abstract morality it is clear that the deeds of Ohlendorf and his Einsatzgruppe D and the deeds of the 393d Bombardment Squadron are parallel, in that in both cases noncombatant enemy civilians were slaughtered. It is true that the Nazi policy was in itself much more evil than the Allied policy of bombing noncombatants both because the former was responsible for the slaughter of millions whereas the victims of the latter were numbered merely in the hundreds of thousands, and because the Nazi policy was clearly genocidal in intent. It is true also that the action of the American bombardier was impersonal; he pressed a button and did not even see his victims. And such impersonal action does not convey the same horror to the imagination as the action of the Nazi who shot his victim face to face and watched him die in agony. However, these differences are accidental. The essential fact is that both Ohlendorf's men and the men of the 393d Bombardment Squadron killed without justification—they were literally murderers. The parallel is inescapable.

Why, then, do Americans in general judge so differently the slaughter of the Jews by the Nazis and the slaughter of noncombatants by the Allies? Why is the usual judgment of the two men ultimately responsible for these slaughters so different? The memory of Hitler is detested; he is thought of as an almost subhuman savage. On the other hand, Truman remains a respected citizen. The minions of Hitler were condemned as common criminals. The more prominent among their leaders were tried at Nuremberg and put to death. Yet the members of the 393d Bombardment Squadron are treated as the honorable veterans of a great war. At their reunions they discuss their deed at Hiroshima without embarrassment with newspaper reporters and pose for photographs.[11]

If Americans in general judge so radically differently the Nazi policy of genocide and the American policy of bombing noncombatants, there can be only one possible explanation. Their moral judgments are based on something other than sound ethics or moral theology. They are based either on emotions or on sophisms which conceal the truth; they are based, in the terminology of the present chapter, on the ethic of respectability. This is a fact to fill one with the utmost horror; for unless man can learn to guide his societal life by some higher principle, one can predict with certainty that the history of the future will be filled with stories of mass slaughter, persecution, and the exploitation of the weak. Against such evils, the development of a sound social ethic is the only defense.

7

The Ethic of Christian Love

WE have shown examples of certain immoral social mores, how these mores had the tacit or explicit approval of the mass of respectable citizens of their time and place, and the consequences of abiding by these mores. However, calling these mores evil implied some criterion. Our criterion has been the Christian law of charity, which we will now discuss explicitly and at length.

Possiby the chief obstacle to the understanding of Christian charity is its seeming simplicity. To say that man's supreme duty is to love God and his neighbor may sound too pat to be convincing. Yet the reality is not obvious; not the greatest contemplative saints could boast of understanding it fully. To obtain even an elementary insight into the nature of Christian love requires long and intense consideration.

There is no better way to begin than with the well-known words of Christ Himself as recounted in the tenth chapter of St. Luke's Gospel. A certain lawyer, that is, an expert in the Jewish Law, put a question to our Lord, "Master, what must I do to obtain eternal life?"

Christ returned the question to the lawyer, "What is written in the Law? How does it read?"

The lawyer answered, "Love the Lord your God with your whole heart and with your whole soul, and with your whole strength, and with your whole mind; and your neighbor as yourself."

Christ approved. "Your answer is correct," he said. "Do this and you will live."

It is interesting to note that the lawyer quoted from the Old Testament and that Christ approved the quotation as a rule of life for Christianity.[1] It was in this sense that He came not to abolish the Law or the Prophets, but to fulfill them.[2] It is therefore important not to exaggerate the contrast between Judaism and Christianity. Both have preached, as man's most basic obligation, the duty of universal love.

But to return to the lawyer—he was finding the situation somewhat embarrassing; for it was now apparent that he had known the answer to the question all along and that he had not asked it in good faith. So he quickly shifted to another question, "And who is my neighbor?" Our Lord's answer was the extraordinary parable of the Good Samaritan.

There are several often overlooked points to be noted about this parable. It is important to realize, first of all, that it illustrates the minimum standard, not the ideal. The question was about what one *must* do to obtain eternal life, and the answer was that one *must* practice charity according to the example of the Good Samaritan. Whoever fails to meet this minimum standard cannot hope for heaven. Charity is not a work of supererogation. It is the very essence of the Christian life. If the question had been about perfection instead of about the minimum standard, doubtless our Lord would have answered with what He said to the rich young man. "If you want to be perfect, go, sell your property and give to the poor, and you will have treasure in heaven; then come, follow me."[3] A second frequently overlooked point is that the Samaritan proved his love genuine not primarily by *feeling* something but by *doing* something. It is true that love is quite usually accompanied by emotion; but emotion is not of its essence and proves very little. Genuine love resides in the will and is directed towards the well-being of the beloved; genuine love must therefore show its quality by active efforts towards this goal. The priest and the Levite could have helped the wounded man, but did not; certainly, then, they could not be said to love him. The Samaritan loved and *therefore* acted.

Finally, the Samaritan loved across an ethnic barrier. The enmity of the Jews for his people was traditional. Two centuries earlier, the Son of Sirach had written:

> My soul loathes two nations
> and the third is not even a people:
> Those who live in Seir and the Philistines
> and the foolish folk who dwell in Sichem.[4]

Thus the author hated the Samaritans of Sichem as he hated the Edomites and Philistines. In the time of Christ the same feeling prevailed. "Jews have no dealings with Samaritans."[5] This enmity had a long history. After the fall of Israel in 722 B.C., Sargon of Assyria had exiled some of the Jews living there and had replaced the deportees with a mixture of captives from various pagan nations.[6] The Jews and the new arrivals gradually intermarried, and their cults, too, became mixed. The Jews of our Lord's day looked down upon the Samaritans with contempt as a mongrelized people who had degraded the pure worship of God and the pure blood of Israel with a pagan admixture—a contempt very similar to that displayed by Hitler's genocidal underlings and white southern racists today. The Good Samaritan knew this, of course, but he acted nevertheless.

The lesson of the parable of the Good Samaritan is clear, simple, and direct. To attain "salvation," we must not merely love God, but we must love our neighbor with a love that expresses itself in deeds. We must be willing to make sacrifices, to take trouble and incur expense, to promote our neighbor's well-being. Finally, we must love *all* our neighbors, regardless of their origins or personal characteristics.

The passages just quoted leave one obvious question unanswered. Religion is essentially the loving service of almighty God; how, then, does it also involve the loving service of one's neighbor? The two duties seem to be considered in some sense identical, and it is not immediately clear why this is the case.

Some light is thrown on the question by the description of the Last Judgment in the twenty-fifth chapter of St. Matthew's Gospel. It is a highly dramatic description. The Son of man, attended by all the angels, will seat Himself on the throne of judgment. Before Him, all nations will be assembled. He will separate them into two groups "just as a shepherd separates the sheep from the goats." He will say to those on the right: "Come, O blessed of my Father. Take possession of the kingdom prepared for you from the foundation of the world; for I was hungry and you gave me to eat, I was thirsty and you gave me to drink, I was a stranger and you received me as a guest, I was without clothes and you clothed me, I was sick and you visited me, I was in prison and you came to see me."

To this the just will reply with questions: "Lord, when did we see you hungry and feed you, or thirsty and give you to drink? When did we see you a stranger and receive you as a guest, or see you without clothes and clothe you? When did we see you sick or in prison and come to visit you?"[7]

Then the King will answer: "I tell you truly, inasmuch as you did it to one of these least of my brethren, you did it to me."

The wicked will be judged by the application of the same principle. They showed no love for their neighbors in need and thus they proved that they had no real love for Christ. "Inasmuch as you did not do it to one of these least ones, neither did you do it to me."

Here, then, is the answer to the question posed above about the relation between the loving service of God and the loving service of neighbor. Surprisingly enough, the relation turns out to be an identity. Serving one's neighbor *is* serving God in men who are His images. To give food or drink or clothing to the poor is to give them to Christ. This is true even of service to prisoners. A man in jail does not seem to be a very good representative of our Lord. He is, nevertheless, inasmuch as his character as an image of God is ineradicable. Note that the statement is not limited to prisoners who happen to be, in fact, guiltless. It is quite general. One must be prepared to see Christ in *all* men. Charity must be universal or it is not charity.

The two Gospel passages which we have quoted define the dimensions of Christian charity. We must, as a minimum, love all men without distinction, we must show our love by helping them in practical ways in their day-by-day necessities, and we must be motivated by the realization that our love for the humblest of our neighbors is the measure of our love for Christ. This duty is not presented as an ideal for rare heroic souls. It is the simple duty of the everyday Christian.

Charity is the *essential* Christian virtue; it is the only virtue necessary for salvation. It is easy to see why this is so. He who has charity loves God and therefore will not sin against God; he loves his neighbor and therefore will not sin against his neighbor; he loves himself supernaturally and therefore will not degrade himself by sin. Moreover, since charity is a single virtue, he who acts charitably in one way, say, by helping his neighbor, proves that he is willing to practice charity in other ways when the occasion arises. Thus St. Paul could write, "He who loves his neighbor has fulfilled the Law."[8] Thus, too, it is easy to understand why in the twenty-fifth chapter of St. Matthew men are judged solely on their willingness to practice the corporal works of mercy. By these deeds they proved that they possessed charity; and that was enough to merit heaven.

The Christian social ideal is simply a society controlled by the law of charity, the ethic of Christian love. This is the premise of all the Church's social teaching. This is presupposed by all the social encyclicals. This is illustrated very excellently in the lives of the saints.

One cannot but be struck by a clear contrast between the Christian life as it is presented theoretically in many books of asceticism and as it is illustrated practically by the way the saints lived. The ascetical literature emphasizes prayer and

131

penance. The saints also emphasized prayer and penance in their lives; but to this they added a third element, the practice of the works of mercy.[9] Even the cloistered saints shared this concern for their neighbor's welfare, and they prayed unceasingly for him. Service of one's neighbor has an extraordinarily sanctifying effect. This is true not only in the case of the saints, but also in the case of ordinary Catholics. Wherever people gather together to serve the poor in a direct personal way, at the cost of self-sacrifice, they find holiness. This is evident in the Catholic Worker and Friendship House groups in New York and elsewhere and in Washington's Fides House with which the present writer was long associated. The way to be a good Christian is simply to serve one's neighbor in need.

If charity is beautiful, then lack of charity is correspondingly abominable. Not only hatred, but even a careless disregard of one's neighbor and his necessities is enough to deserve damnation. Those condemned to hell in that terrible twenty-fifth chapter of St. Matthew did not, apparently, really hate their needy neighbors. They were simply too busy with their own selfish lives to care about them. Obviously, then, a mere lack of concern for human suffering is itself damnable.[10]

It is very hard to find an excuse for those who call themselves Christians and who yet consistently refuse to face realistically the problems of the subproletariat. It is almost impossible to imagine the muffling of conscience in a man who votes against a fair-housing law or who refuses to hire a worker on account of race; it is almost impossible to imagine how he can reconcile his conduct with the exigent law of Christian love. The middle-class American who talks glibly about the "shiftlessness" and the "immorality" of slum dwellers and who opposes adequate relief budgets for them would seem to express quite clearly the attitudes of those who will hear on Judgment Day the words, "Inasmuch as you did not do it to one of these least ones, neither did you do it to me."

But if a mere callousness towards one's neighbor is damnable, what can be said of those who actively hate others and who persecute and destroy them? This is a degree of evil which is simply diabolical; yet it is a degree of evil which frequently controls national policy with the cooperation of the respectable. This fact is illustrated by examples discussed in this book; but these are merely examples; it would be very easy to multiply instances of the callous exploitation or cruel persecution of the defenseless by the respectable holders of power.

Of course, it is extremely unfair to judge the personal guilt of any individual who may have acted in what he misguidedly thinks to be good faith. Indeed, there is reason to believe, for example, that many slaveholders actually did live with clear consciences. What is shocking is not the personal guilt of those responsible for the major crimes of society; for that is something we cannot know. What is shocking is the objective evil of their policies and of the systematic long-term erosion of conscience which tolerated them.

It ought to be a subject of endless meditation from the bishops down to the ordinary laymen that Catholics participated in the formation and execution of the national policies criticized in this book, policies which were—objectively speaking—the very anti-

133

thesis of Christian charity. Catholics, lay persons, priests, religious, and bishops held slaves and defended slavery in the United States. Catholics supported Hitler's war, and the slaughter of the Jews was part of his war policy. Catholics were as active as their fellow Americans in the massacre of noncombatants during the Second World War.

One fact emerges very clearly from the foregoing discussion. To be charitable, one must often be disobedient. To acquiesce in slavery or genocide or—worse still—to take an active part in the execution of such policies is certainly to sin very grievously against charity; it is to be un-Christian to the uttermost. Disobedience is the necessary alternative. The good Christian cannot conform to the mores of a paramoral society. He must make it clear by both words and actions that he rejects these mores. By doing so, of course, he will exclude himself from the ranks of those who are considered "respectable." He may become an outcast. In some instances his opposition may cost him his liberty or even his life.

The supreme example of a refusal to conform to evil mores and of the personal cost of that refusal is given by our Lord Himself. He attacked the respectable classes of the time for their vices and thus earned their bitter hatred. When the danger of this position became evident, He did not relent. On the contrary, He continued the attack. The crucifixion was the final result of the power structure's hatred for Him.

Thus, Christ attacked the rich. "How hard it will be," He remarked one day, "for those who have riches to enter the kingdom of God."[11] This indictment of the most respectable segment of society struck His hearers as shocking. "The disciples were dumbfounded at his words." However, instead of modifying the statement, Christ reinforced it. "It is easier for a camel to get through the eye of a needle than for a rich man to enter the kingdom of God." There are, indeed, exceptions. Joseph of Arimathea and Zaccheus are explicitly called "rich," yet they were virtuous men. This, however, must be ascribed to the special grace of God with whom "all things are possible"—even the salvation of the wealthy. What our Lord was condemning in the passage quoted —and what is condemned elsewhere in the New Testament— seems to be not so much the mere possession of wealth as the obsessive pursuit of gain. Some passages give information about the financial background of those spoken of as "rich." They seem to have been merchants, farmer-capitalists, and those who might roughly be called financiers, that is, persons such as bankers or tax collectors who dealt directly with money.[12] All were actively seeking financial success.

Christ did not hesitate to show disdain for civil authorities when they deserved it. On being told that Herod Antipas wanted to kill Him, He referred to this powerful ruler as "that fox."[13] The word implies a knavish craftiness and is the only example of "unmitigated *contempt* (as distinguished from rebuke and scorn) recorded among the utterances of Christ."[14] Later, when brought before Herod in the course of the Passion, He further showed His contempt by refusing even to speak to him.[15]

The bitter denunciation of the scribes and Pharisees by our Lord must have created a profound sensation. These men were not only powerful; they passed as models of righteousness. If

135

any group in the country was looked up to as eminently respectable, surely it was this group. Yet Christ's language in reference to them was extreme. To realize just how much so, one has only to reread the twenty-third chapter of St. Matthew's Gospel, where these representatives of the power structure are called "hypocrites," "blind guides," "blind fools," "serpents," "brood of vipers." They are denounced as obstacles to the spread of the Kingdom, as petty casuists who pervert the moral law, as murderers of God's envoys. Outwardly, in the eyes of men, they appear righteous, but within they are full of iniquity. "How," Christ demanded of them, "can you escape being sentenced to hell?"

Certainly, on one, and most probably on two occasions Christ drove a group of respectable businessmen out of the Temple.[16] Apparently, there were quite a few of them. Some were merchants who offered for sale the sheep and oxen needed for sacrifice. Others sold doves to be used as offerings by the poor. Others were money-changers who furnished the shekels needed for the temple tax in exchange for foreign coins.

If Jesus had merely denounced these practices, that itself would have been very dramatic. However, He went beyond words. "He made a lash out of cords," St. John tells us, "and drove all the men out of the Temple, the sheep, too, and the oxen; and he scattered the coin of the money-changers and overturned their tables."[17] This physical violence, this public humiliation must have infuriated the merchants. It also infuriated "the chief priests and the scribes." By invading the Temple precincts, Christ had trespassed on their prerogatives. St. Mark, in his account of the incident, states that these latter then plotted to kill Him. However, they had to restrain their anger because the crowd was on his side.[18]

Quite clearly, Christ was threatening the privileges of the respectable classes, the rich, the influential, the religious leaders. He did not stop at words. He made scenes; that is, like many civil-rights advocates today He "demonstrated." He had, moreover, a popular following, which, if it were allowed to increase, might cause a social upheaval in which the respectable would be unmasked. The obvious thing to do—as has been done in the South today—was to put the "radical" to death. However, His enemies had to bide their time. They had to plan carefully. Finally, however, the propitious moment came and they struck. Christ was dragged before Pilate.

It is illuminating to examine the immediate causes of the crucifixion. It was, in the first instance, the judicial murder of one who had earned the hatred of the privileged classes; and so it is not surprising that the indictment which was brought forward when Christ stood before Pilate emphasized the fact that He was an agitator.

> We have found this man perverting our nation,
> and forbidding the payment of taxes to the emperor,
> and claiming to be Christ, a king.[19]

Of course, these charges were false and misleading; Christ certainly did not oppose the payment of taxes. But His messiahship was made to appear as implying the seizure of civil power. However, the charge of "perverting our nation" betrays the fact that the accusers were worried about the effect of Christ's social teaching. When Pilate remained unimpressed by these charges, the accusers renewed their indictment.

> He stirs up the people, teaching throughout all
> Judea, from Galilee even to this place.[20]

To stir up is to agitate and demonstrate. Christ was a social agitator for what today would be called "human rights." He threatened the existing state of affairs. To the privileged classes, this was intolerable.

Christ's denunciation of the privileged classes illustrates the contrast between the ethic of respectability and the ethic of Christian love; but it does more. It shows that charity can be denunciatory and violent as well as gentle and meek. Christ showed charity towards the woman taken in adultery by being very kind and tactful with her.[21] However, His denunciation of the scribes and Pharisees was also an act of charity—and this because, first, the only hope of making these hypocrites realize their true condition was to jolt their consciences by strong and candid language; and secondly—and more importantly—because these false teachers were corrupting the people by their perversion of the moral law, and the only way to lessen their pernicious influence was to expose them. This was an act of charity towards His hearers. Acts of fraternal charity, viewed externally, differ vastly among themselves. What unifies them is the fact that they are all directed towards the well-being of one's neighbor.

It is a mistake to overemphasize Christian meekness as it has, in high and low places, often been overemphasized. It even happens that a false and degenerate Christian art will picture Christ as weak and effeminate—which is, of course blasphemy in the strict theological sense. It is true that Christ told His followers to turn the other cheek; but He also proclaimed that He came not to bring peace, but the sword.[22] Meekness is only one Christian virtue; perfection consists in the combination of all the virtues in harmony.

Charity can be defined alternatively as the following of Christ. Thus not only His words, but also His deeds, constitute a lesson for mankind. His way of acting under various circumstances shows man how he too should act when similar circumstances arise in his own life. Of course, one imitates Christ by living quietly and unobtrusively as He did at Nazareth, by quietly facing the duties of each successive day and performing them to the best of one's ability, by living modestly and temperately as a good Christian citizen.

There are times, however, when the follower of Christ must go beyond these everyday duties. If he lives in a paramoral society, if he sees his fellow human being deceived or exploited or enslaved or massacred, then love of neighbor must manifest itself by public protest or by a brave disobedience to unjust laws, when the occasion arises. Under such circumstances, it is un-Christian to hold one's tongue for fear of being thought eccentric or to refrain from action for fear of punishment. "Christ himself suffered for you, leaving you an example so that you might follow his footsteps."[23]

8

The Strong Delusion

IT is apparent that the great injustices of history, the exploitations of the defenseless, the massacres of the innocent, the savage persecutions, are perpetrated not by disreputable men who disobey good laws, but by respectable men who obey evil laws. If the modern world is far from the Christian ideal of a society dominated by holy charity, if it falls much short even of the natural ideal of a society in which justice is respected, then the chief explanation is not to be found in the crimes of lawless men. They constitute only a minor factor. The chief explanation is to be found in the structural injustices built into paramoral societies, the injustices consecrated by the mores, approved by the leading citizens, and sanctioned by an ethic of respectability.

The Federal Bureau of Investigation reported 9,250 victims of murder or nonnegligent manslaughter in the United States for 1964. On the average there was a murder an hour during the year.[1] This is not only appalling; it is a matter for deep national shame. Any citizen must be disgusted to the point of nausea at the presence in this nation of so many criminals morally degraded to the point of willful and unjustified taking of human life.

But if 9,250 is a large number, it is less than one-seventh of 68,000, the total slaughtered at Hiroshima, less than one ninth of the 83,793 massacred at Tokyo, less than one-fourteenth of the 135,000 brutally slain at Dresden. Yet these killings were ordered and carried out by persons considered to be respectable and honored as such.

It has been estimated that during the three and a half centuries of the Atlantic slave trade thirty or forty million Negroes died in slave raids, coffles, or barracoons.[2] Yet the slavery which caused this prodigious slaughter had the support of public opinion, with only occasional and ineffective protest. Slavery was accepted as part of the mores in the United States and in many other countries of the hemisphere. It was respectable to keep slaves—indeed, it marked a particularly high degree of respectability—even though the system had the murders of the Atlantic slave trade as its necessary basis.

Criminals kill by the thousand; decent and respectable citizens kill by the hundred thousand or the million.

When we speak of "decent and respectable" citizens, we do not speak ironically. The tragic and mysterious aspect of the phenomenon lies precisely in this, that many of those responsible for these repeated outrages seem clearly to have been upright men. Of the slaveholders of the Old South, some, doubtless, were evil. On the average, however, they were simply the solid citizens of the community. Moreover, some among them were men of outstanding civic virtue, and it was the support of such outstanding citizens that made the system of slavery impregnable. There were men like Washington and Jefferson who risked their fortunes and even their lives for the high purpose of founding a nation to be governed by the concept of human freedom. These were men of intelligence and broad culture, men upright and conscientious in their personal lives. Yet these men held slaves. Even more surprising, perhaps, are the slaveholders among the early priests and religious. They bravely professed the faith in a predominantly hostile environment; they lived rugged, sacrificing lives for the sake of their vocation; they were holy, selfless, generous in their virtue. But they were also slaveholders.

This blindness to social evil can affect any generation, including our own. Many Americans today are quite blind to the immorality of the obliteration bombing of noncombatants in the last world war. They are blind to its use in the Vietnamese "political action" now being waged. Americans are as blind to the evil of noncombatant bombing as men of the Old South were to the evil of slavery. Yet from the objective standpoint of moral theology there can be no doubt at all that the bombing of Hiroshima—or any unjust bombing of civilian areas—is precisely what Pope Paul VI called "an outrage against civilization."

There is something even more appalling than the failure of so many to understand the immorality of a specific policy such as the deliberate bombing of noncombatants. This is the very widespread failure to regard war as a moral issue at all. The present writer has lived through two world wars and what is most disturbing is the fact that in both of them people usually accepted every act of war as justified without discussion. To them, the morality of war was simply not debatable. During both wars there were some conscientious objectors. Whether one agrees with their conclusions or not—personally, we ourself did agree— the fact remains that these men were most certainly right in their conviction that war is a moral problem that must be grappled with. Doubtless, there were other men, equally sincere, who also faced the moral issue, decided that the war was just, and enlisted. However, it seems clear that the total in both groups was quite small. In all the literature one read, in all the speeches one heard, in all the private conversations one listened to, the morality of the war was almost always taken for granted without discussion.

If decent and respectable citizens support immoral laws and immoral policies, at least part of the trouble is sheer ignorance.

To reach a practical moral judgment about a particular action, two premises must be established. First, a general moral principle must be demonstrated. Secondly, it must be proved that the particular action at issue falls under the stated principle. Thus one might argue,

Direct killing of noncombatants is a grave violation of natural law.

But the bombing of Dresden in 1945 was direct killing of noncombatants.

Therefore the bombing of Dresden in 1945 was a grave violation of natural law.

In every discussion of social morality, propositions of both these types must sooner or later be involved. Even if a premise is not stated explicitly, it will be clearly implied by the nature of the argument. This is quite inescapable.

But the two sorts of premises are drawn from two quite different groups of disciplines. Moral principles come from ethics or moral theology. The empirical facts come from history, sociology, psychology, economics, or some other discipline that deals with actual human society. It is important to bear in mind that the two groups of disciplines have quite different methods and call for quite different skills. Perhaps this is one reason why much discussion of social morality is so unclear and indecisive. If any premise is weak, the conclusion must be weak. A general who discusses military policy on the naïve assumption that any successful strategy is by that fact permissible is bound to reach scandalous conclusions; and a moral theologian exiles his speculations to the limbo of irrelevance if he treats intergroup problems without an exact knowledge of the nature of these problems and of their current extent. It must be clear that both moralists and social scientists have something essential to contribute; if either group works ineffectively, a morally confused public policy will be the inevitable result.

If respectable citizens thoughtlessly follow the mores of a paramoral society, some of the blame must therefore fall on the intellectuals. In our complex modern world nonspecialists have no choice but to rely on specialists for help. Obviously, a bridge cannot be built without the guidance of an engineer; only a surgeon is competent to remove an appendix; it needs a highly skilled crew to fly a transatlantic jet. Yet to both moralists and students of the social sciences it is not always equally self-evident that to make sound judgments about the values of contemporary society also calls for specialized training and skill and mutual respect for each other's disciplines. The two basic disciplines here involved will now be discussed, together with possible reasons for their ineffectiveness: the moral disciplines will be taken up first, then the empirical social sciences.

In the present day there seems to be comparatively little interest in a systematic science of morality. That is to say, there seems to be little interest in the disciplines whose purpose is to set up general moral norms and then to argue deductively from these to specific tenets applying to a particular area of human activity. This does not mean that this age is indifferent to morality or that it lacks moral earnestness. It means only that morality tends to be based on emotion, on unexamined premises, on group spirit, rather than on an intellectual examination of principles. That is, of course, a very broad statement, yet there is reason to believe it true.

Past ages have produced ethical systems which were very influential in the formation of public policy. One may think, for example, of Chinese Confucianism, of the Stoicism of the classical age, of the medieval Scholastic synthesis, or of the natural-rights theories of the eighteenth century. Each of these had a long and complicated history and was the result of much rational effort by serious and committed thinkers. These systems were all very different; yet they had one element in common. They all reflected the conviction that man, using his reason, taking facts naturally available to him and perhaps also facts supernaturally revealed, could build a logically sound, intellectually defensible system of morality. Possibly this conviction is weak in the present age; possibly this age lacks the necessary ethical sophistication. And perhaps this is one reason why respectable citizens can approve outrageous public policies without realizing what they are doing.

Whatever may be said of the general spirit of the age, it is abundantly clear that at least Catholics profess to take ethics and moral theology seriously. In Catholic colleges ethics has a respected place and is quite usually a required course; in seminaries future priests take four years of moral theology; moreover, Catholic books and periodicals are constantly appearing with both popular and technical discussions of every conceivable moral question. Obviously, then, Catholics are very much in earnest about discussing morality. Yet Catholics did not protest very vociferously or effectively against Negro slavery in America, against Hitler's wars in Germany, or against the bombing of noncombatants in the Second World War—to cite only those instances treated above. How Catholics can devote so much time and effort to the study of the moral sciences and yet fail to recognize obvious and large-scale affronts to everything that those sciences imply is a question that demands answering.

To understand the spirit of Catholic moral theology, one must grasp its relation to the sacrament of penance. Seminarians are taught morality so that later, as confessors, they can pass judgment on what penitents tell them. This usually means passing judgment on series of specific acts and omissions. This is the sort of thing that one is expected to mention in confession, as is evident from the standard forms for the examination of conscience available in prayer books and elsewhere. "Have I neglected my morning and night prayers? . . . Have I taken God's name in vain? . . . Have I deliberately missed Mass? . . . Have I taken pleasure in impure thoughts or desires? . . . Have I stolen? . . . Have I told lies?" Not surprisingly, this same preoccupation with the specific shows up in the technical literature. In recent issues of *The American Ecclesiastical Review* a distinguished moral theologian answered the following questions, among others. May an Episcopalian clergyman be called a "priest"? May Catholics patronize a drugstore in which contraceptives are sold? May a used-car dealer repair a car so as to give the impression that it is in better condition than it actually is? If two good Catholics are eating in a restaurant on a day of abstinence and one inadvertently orders meat, must the other remind him of the day?[3]

Moral theology is dominated by a concern with concrete instances. It would be fair to call it casuistical, were it not that this word has acquired a pejorative meaning which implies superficiality and sophistry. To avoid this unfair implication, it would be better to say that moral theology is *act-oriented*. In this it differs from ascetical theology, for example, which is less concerned with particular actions than with general personality trends, with habits and attitudes such as the spirit of prayer or detachment from worldly goods. It is concerned with the sort of person one is. It may therefore be called *actor-oriented*.

The distinction between the two approaches may be illustrated by the contrast between the old-fashioned criminal court and the modern socialized court. The former was act-oriented. It was concerned only with the question of whether the defendant had committed a specific offense, and if he was found guilty, with the imposition of a punishment. If he was found not guilty, the court had no further concern about him. In contrast to this, a socialized court is actor-oriented. For example, in a modern juvenile court, at least ideally, the most important issue is not the question of whether a boy committed a specific offense; rather, the court is concerned primarily with the boy himself. Is he the type of child who is likely to become an adult criminal? If so, what can be done to help him? A child may need such help even though he has violated no law. The focus of attention is the child himself.

Because moral theology is act-oriented, it emphasizes particularly those sins which are clear-cut offenses, sins such as stealing, lying, missing Mass on Sunday, and, above all, sexual sins. The latter are ideal material for the act-oriented approach because they are definite mental events or definite external acts which are so emotionally charged that they cannot be easily overlooked. The result is, as we know, that sexual sins receive an enormous emphasis in Catholic thought. In itself, of course, this may be all to the good. However, a preoccupation with this particular area can lead to an irrational prudery and it can also distract attention from more important issues. The Catholic diocesan press has recently been carrying a great deal of detailed news about campaigns against pornography; but there has been little or no serious discussion about the morality of the war in Vietnam or about particular aspects of that war such as the alleged napalm bombing of inhabited villages.

The act-oriented approach is not very effective in defining the individual's duties in certain areas that are of grave importance socially. The sin of avarice offers a highly relevant example. Christ Himself made it clear that the rich find it very difficult to attain heaven; and St. Paul stated comprehensively, "The love of money is the root of all evils."[4] It is clear that a preoccupation with material things, an excessive attachment to one's own possessions, coupled with a hard-hearted indifference to the poverty of others, is a contradiction of fundamental Christian ideals. But where, precisely, does one make the choice between God and mammon? What is the dividing line between a prudent concern for one's financial responsibilities and that gloating devotion to material things that distracts one from God and results in injury to one's neighbor? It is not enough to preach detachment as a counsel of perfection. It is a task of moral theology to identify sin. Society is to be reformed not merely by appealing to the generosity of the generous, but also by threats of punishment to wrongdoers. The reluctant Catholic must be told precisely what he *must* do if he is not to be corrupted by avarice.

Similarly, act-oriented theology is not very helpful in the complex field of race relations. One may take, for example, the case of a sincere Catholic who happens to be an influential citizen in a Mississippi town that is riddled with racial injustices. Negroes are paid on a wage scale of their own, much lower than the white scale. They do not receive equal justice in the courts. Their side of town has unpaved and poorly lighted streets, inadequate sewerage and water supply. And so on through the whole gamut of customary maltreatment. Under such circumstances there are many laudable things the Catholic might do: he might write letters to the local newspaper and to his representatives in the state legislature; he might contribute money to civil-rights movements; he might use his personal influence with local officials; he might do these and much besides. However, the question now is: What *must* he do as a matter of strict obligation? What are his exact duties as a Catholic? Precisely how must he act to avoid mortal sin? If moral theology cannot answer these questions satisfactorily, a man is likely to conclude that, since he has no definable obligations, he has no obligations whatever. Undefined duties are not a sharp spur to conscience.

Recently, there has been a trend towards the development of a more actor-oriented moral theology, whose most prominent spokesman has been the distinguished Redemptorist, Father Bernard Häring,[5] in whose view moral theology should be very much more than a catalogue of commands and prohibitions. This is a promising trend; however, to meet the need discussed here, the new moral theology will have to do more than describe the sort of person a Christian *should* be. It will have to describe what he *must* be.

Nevertheless, moral theology has sometimes been used very successfully in making the Christian social ideal more concrete. Father John La Farge did much more than talk about interracial justice in general; he applied general principles to the concrete Negro-white situation in the United States. In the field of economics Msgr. John A. Ryan was equally specific, and he greatly influenced contemporary thought on labor relations and in many other fields. It would be possible to name many others whose work made the Christian social ideal more concrete. Of course, the activities of all these men have simply been a part of the modern Catholic social movement which is rooted in the great social encyclicals and has been expressed in many, many forms of social action in various countries around the world.

To summarize the present discussion, it seems fair to state that Catholic theology has been vastly more successful in defining the social ideal than in defining sins against it. Devotion to the ideal has inspired very many lay people, priests, and religious to make sacrifices in the service of their neighbors and in the whole field of social action. Yet the definition of the individual's obligations has been so imprecise that sincere Catholics could participate in Hitler's war with untroubled consciences or could approve the slaughter of noncombatants by the Allies. They could participate in the savage wrongs committed against Negroes in the United States from the days of the Atlantic slave trade, through the dreary history of slavery, down to the contemporary violation of justice in segregation. Something is manifestly wrong.

If the moralists have often failed to condemn serious social evils, their failure can be explained in large measure by their lack of access to the relevant facts. Often they have been simply unaware of what was going on. A very clear example is furnished by slavery in the Old South where it was widely accepted that the Negro was biologically inferior, that he was incapable of managing his own affairs, that slavery in America was a step upward from African "savagery," and that the slaves were on the whole content. Given such premises, it is not very surprising that moral theologians were very mild in their criticism of American slavery.

It is hard to understand how sincere and intelligent men in the slave states could have been so blind. Of course, they did not share the modern anthropologist's knowledge of the high and complex cultures of West Africa; but they must have known that there were well-organized Negro states there whose rulers dealt as equals or superiors with the white slave traders. If such sincere men felt that Negroes were ineducable, why did the slave codes have to forbid teaching them to read and write or giving them books or pamphlets? How could it be said that slaves were contented when such elaborate precautions had to be taken to prevent their escape? It is true that slaves usually found it expedient to conceal their real feelings; nevertheless, if any white man sincerely wanted to know the truth, there must have been many like Frederick Douglass who would have been glad to tell him. This perverse blindness to the facts was doubtless the chief reason why the immorality of slavery was not seen in its naked ugliness.

In the century since the Emancipation Proclamation a great deal of intellectual progress has been made. No reputable scientist would now argue that the Negro is genetically inferior in intellectual, artistic, or social abilities. A vast mass of statistics is available to show the correlation between discrimination on the one hand and Negro health, education, employment, income, and housing on the other. Yet in spite of all this very little is known about the more intimate effects on personality of the myriad varieties of Negro-white adjustment across the wide spectrum of contemporary society. To realize this, one has only to read such a book as Claude Brown's autobiography, *Manchild in the Promised Land*.[6] The culture of Harlem as he describes it is something clearly distinct from the standard American culture. It is a way of life, a system of values, an organizational complex that is quite alien and unfamiliar to most other

152

citizens. The two cultures have certain superficial resemblances, of course, but this fact is likely to lead one to overlook their basic differences. To the average American the culture of Harlem is not much more understandable than the culture of the Incas of Peru.

The culture of Harlem is only one of the many subproletarian cultures which exist in modern America. The fact of racial segregation adds something distinctive to those subsections of American society whose members are colored. However, the subproletariat, colored or white, is always distinctive. This point has been stressed in an earlier chapter. It is referred to again at this point to illustrate the fact that moral judgments can be warped by a lack of factual knowledge. If men appear apathetic when face-to-face with social injustice, it is often because they do not know enough about the situation to see their duty clearly. This fact was brought home strongly by the experience of the Bureau of Social Research at Catholic University in evaluating the work of a number of experimental and demonstration projects which were set up with government funds to train hard-core unemployed youths and place them in suitable jobs.[7] In spite of generous funds, intelligence, energy, and enthusiasm, the personnel of the projects found their task unexpectedly difficult. To the present writer, the essence of the difficulty seemed to be the characteristic white-collar ignorance of the sociology and psychology of the subproletariat.

In all honesty, one must admit that the social sciences have over the years accumulated only a very meager store of helpful knowledge. It would be easy to cite many illustrations of this fact, for example their failure to attain enough insight into the causes of crime and delinquency to yield any real help in the control of these evils. However, it is unnecessary to labor the point. Engineers know how to build good roads, public-health experts know how to control typhoid, but sociologists do not know how to prevent future Watts-type riots. It is well and good to channel federal funds into distressed areas. However, such palliative measures do not touch the basic difficulty, the sad dichotomy between a Negro, subproletarian culture and the culture of the white bourgeoisie. The dichotomy is old and bitter. Its roots are deep. Its effects reach down into the unplumbed, unconscious depth of human personality. Sociology and psychology can thus far give only a most superficial and generalized explanation of what happened at Watts.

If the behavioral and social sciences are not very successful in throwing light on problems such as those just mentioned, one reason is their failure to attract the country's best scholars. Elbridge Sibley, in a critical study of the education of sociologists, has shown that this is one of the major handicaps existing in that field.[8] A study of Graduate Record Examination quantitative aptitude scores revealed, for example, that in competitive tests for the National Program for Graduate School Selection, 1955–57, sociology candidates ranked fifteenth among sixteen fields, and education candidates were sixteenth.[9] Sociology is the most general of the sciences studying social behavior and the discipline known as "education" ought to be responsible for the efficient transmission of knowledge to succeeding generations. Both must occupy key positions in a strategy to build a better society, but it is obvious that they cannot unless they attract the more promising students.

In planning for social reform, it is almost essential to have available some generalizations about group behavior, in other words, some sort of valid social theory.[10] However, what is offered in this field is very unsatisfactory; to make matters worse, it is often expressed in what Pitirim Sorokin rightly calls "obtuse jargon and sham-scientific slang."[11] A great deal of such theory, when translated into English from its characteristic argot, turns out to be either meaningless or trivial. In the very complex field of human behavior it would, of course, be unreasonable to expect generalizations as clear and accurate as those, say, of high-energy physics; however, it would not seem unreasonable to expect something better than what is now being formulated.

When students of society turn away from their theories to do empirical research, the results are usually unimpressive because of certain recurrent faults. One is the tendency to generalize from inadequate samples. Someone studies freshmen at one university and generalizes about all college students; someone studies a few dozen relief clients, social workers, and teachers and draws conclusions about the beliefs of the different social classes; 50 per cent of a group respond to a mail questionnaire and these are assumed to be representative of the entire group.[12] A second fault consists in taking responses to questionnaires at face value. Often questions are worded so broadly that the only realistic response would be, "It all depends." However, even when they are carefully worded, questionnaires are not likely to yield very many valid facts; all the evidence confirms this.[13] Finally, statistical analysis of results is often extremely naïve.

155

Researchers are prone to take intergroup differences at face value without using any statistical norm to determine whether they might not be satisfactorily explained as mere vagaries of chance. Not infrequently, all these faults may be found in the same study, which often shows a lack of scientific rigor that would not be tolerated for an instant in the physical sciences.

The usefulness of the behavioral social sciences in the attack on social evils has been considerably hindered by the contention of some, especially among the sociologists, that their science should be "value-free." If this term means that it is not the social scientist's business to decide questions of social ethics, then it is obviously true. It is obviously true, also, if it means that the scientist's personal values, with their accompanying emotions, should not be allowed to warp his interpretation of research data. However, the principle has been taken to mean that the social scientist must remain aloof from social action and must not use his special skills in the solution of concrete problems. He may, indeed, study intergroup tensions, poverty, prostitution, or drug addiction as interesting social phenomena, but he must study them with a detached attitude. To join the fight against them would be unscientific because this would be to commit himself to the value judgment that they are somehow wrong or abnormal or undesirable.[14]

If the behavioral social sciences were to become value-free in the sense just defined, they would probably be the only sciences to be governed by such a norm. Service to mankind has always been a chief spur to scientific research. Of course, the immediate purpose of the pure scientist is the attainment of truth, which may be on a very abstract level. However, he is very conscious of the fact that abstract truth can have very practical applications, and he is anxious that his own discoveries should be thus applied. To say that sociologists and other social scientists should not be interested in crime control because that would imply a value judgment about crime is just as absurd as to say that a bacteriologist should not be interested in the control of infection because that would imply a value judgment about the undesirability of disease. General speaking, the interplay of pure and applied science has been stimulating to both.[15]

It was an illuminating experience for the present writer to have been at one time a medical student, and at another a graduate student in sociology. The education of future physicians involves very much more than studying textbooks and listening to lectures. Immediately after entering medical school the new student is introduced to the dissecting room. Hour after hour, day after day, month after month, he handles the component parts of the human body, studying their shape, their texture, and their interrelationships. Later, during his clinical years, he deals with patients in the hospital ward and in the operating room, first as an observer and then as a more and more active participant in the process of diagnosis and treatment. This first-hand contact with the problems of disease engenders a very strong sense of personal involvement. The student feels committed to the ideal of providing the very best possible medical care. This sense of commitment makes him willing to accept the heavy work load and the high academic standards which characterize medical education. This education is, of course, oriented primarily towards the needs of practicing physicians; but it is equally well suited to the needs of those who are to devote themselves to pure research. It is, above all, a highly *realistic* education.

In contrast, it is a striking characteristic of sociological education that professors do not usually insist that their students have any first-hand contact with the subject matter they are studying. Taking a course on the community does not usually mean visiting various types of communities, interviewing community members, and observing community life and action. Usually, it means listening to some lectures and doing some reading. A student of juvenile delinquency may never meet a delinquent, see a juvenile court in action, visit a state training school, or study at first hand the characteristics of a high-delinquency neighborhood. Generally speaking, field work plays only a very minor and incidental role in sociological education. Thus it is no exaggeration to say that the major emphasis in the education of sociologists is not the study of society, but the study of books about society.

Graduate students of sociology are expected to learn research principally by fulfilling the thesis requirement, that is, by carrying out some research project and writing it up in a dissertation which may be concerned with theory or with empirical research. However, even if the student chooses the latter, he may still not have any first-hand contact with social reality. His empirical research may involve merely sending out questionnaires or working over statistics gathered from some other source. The dissertation requirement does not make it certain that the student will learn to deal directly with the facts of human society. Therefore, after the new Ph.D. receives his appointment to a university faculty, if he finally decides to study some practical problem at first hand, such as delinquency or intergroup tensions, his research methods may be utterly academic. Under these conditions, it is not surprising that a great deal of sociological research is scientifically defective. What is here asserted in criticism of sociology could probably be applied with almost equal validity to most of the other sciences which study human social behavior. It is always a temptation to turn away from the drudgery of hard-nosed empirical research and take refuge in easily conceived speculative theories.

Fortunately, there is reason to believe that the social sciences may be more practically helpful in the future than they have been in the past. Ever since the passage of the Employment Act of 1946 there has been a systematic attempt to apply the insights of scientific economics to the management of the national economy. The machinery of this application is largely in the hands of the Joint Economic Committee of the Congress and the Council of Economic Advisers. The history of these bodies may be followed in their annual reports and in the annual *Economic Report of the President*. This use of economic science for practical purposes has called forth some criticism. However, it seems fair to concede that the effort has had a good measure of success and—what is more important—that it has illustrated what the social sciences may be able to contribute to the future.[16]

The behavioral social sciences of the future will probably be much different from what they are today. They will conform more closely to the high standards set by the other sciences. This does not mean, as the neo-positivists have imagined, that they

159

must borrow the methods of physics.[17] It does mean, however, that speculative theory will become less and less important and that more and more weight will be given to critically designed empirical studies. It means sophisticated mathematical methods and complex analyses by electronic computer. It means great expense; for if it takes billions of dollars to put a man on the moon it will take more billions to unravel the complex facts of human society with due scientific rigor.

This book has dealt with the great crimes which are perpetrated by organized society under the leadership of respectable citizens. Four such crimes were discussed. It would have been only too easy to multiply examples. Such crimes are the chief obstacle to a good society. Lawless and disreputable men are less responsible than respectable citizens for the major problems of society. Disobedience to good laws in the long run does less harm than obedience to evil laws.

Such crimes are possible only because there exists a *strong delusion* to the effect that what is being done is not wrong, but somehow justifiable. It is the correct thing to do; it is the way to act if one wishes to be considered respectable. Thus there can be a general agreement within the community that chattel slavery constitutes no injustice to the Negro, that it is right and proper to massacre Jews or the civilian inhabitants of enemy cities, or that the misery of the poor is due to their own shiftlessness and is not the responsibility of the community.

Such beliefs constitute a *delusion*. They are a flat contradiction to any valid ethic. The full horror of their acceptance becomes

160

visible, however, only when they are viewed in the light of the ethic of Christian love. The very essence of Christianity, the sole duty of the Christian, is to see Christ in his neighbor, to realize that one's treatment of one's neighbor is the exact measure of one's love for Christ. Even a mere callous neglect of others is damnable, but it is a far worse offense to torture Christ in the person of the slave, the Jew, the enemy noncombatant, the indigent.

Such beliefs constitute a *strong* delusion because they are backed up by the prestige of the respectable. Whoever would oppose slavery in Louisiana was threatened with hanging. Dompropst Lichtenberg spoke up for the Jews and died on his way to a concentration camp. Even when the respectable do not enforce their viewpoint by such extreme measures, it is nevertheless hazardous to oppose it. He who differs with the respectable is automatically suspect. He is not one to be trusted with responsibility. To a greater or lesser degree he finds himself an outcast from respectable society.

In spite of the massive power of the strong delusion, there is still a valid defense against it. This is the power of the human intellect to attain to demonstrable truth. No dictator, no matter how powerful or how cruel, can persuade his subjects that two plus two equals seven. As long as men are serious and diligent in their quest for the truth, so long are they safe from the strong delusion.

If society has suffered so often and so seriously from the strong delusion, it must be that the intellectuals, whose duty it is to lead their fellows in the pursuit of truth, have failed to perform their function satisfactorily. It has been argued in the

161

present chapter that this is indeed the case. More specifically, it has been argued that moralists have been passive in the face of enormous evils and have failed to judge these evils truly, and furthermore that behavioral scientists must share the blame because they have not discovered the relevant facts and have not presented them convincingly. The power of the strong delusion is such that it will not yield to any argument short of moral certitude. If the Christian intellectual, moralist, or social scientist hesitates, he is ineffective.

The strong delusion is today's great challenge to the Christian intellectual; for it is he who has at hand the proper means to overcome it. Society has a great deal to expect from realistic Christian moralists and from scientists who are loyal to a rigorous methodology. It is imperative that these expectations should not be disappointed.

On the Distribution of Income
and the Extent of Poverty

INFORMATION about the distribution of income among families and individuals in the United States is available from several sources. The principal governmental agencies publishing such information are the U.S. Bureau of the Census and the Office of Business Economics, both in the U.S. Department of Commerce. It is important to realize that these two agencies define income differently and gather their information in quite different ways.

The Census has been gathering data about cash income since 1940 as part of the Decennial Census of Population. The method has varied somewhat. In 1960 income questions were asked for each individual member of every fourth household. The Census is also responsible for the Current Population Survey (CPS) in which a random sample of about 35,000 households is interviewed every month for data on employment and other social characteristics. Once a year in March three-quarters of the sample is interviewed for income information. Annual estimates of income distribution appear in a special "Consumer Income" issue of *Current Population Reports*. See Herman P. Miller, *Trends in the Income of Families and Persons in the United States: 1947 to 1960* (Washington, Government Printing Office, 1963) for a wealth of CPS data for the period covered, along with good explanatory discussions. The same author's *Rich Man, Poor Man* (New York, Crowell, 1964) has an excellent appendix, "The Validity of Income Statistics." For a technical account of CPS methods, see U.S. Bureau of the Census, *The Current Population Survey—a Report on Methodology* (Washington, Government Printing Office, 1963).

A second principal governmental source of income statistics is the personal income series of the Office of Business Economics (OBE). This is not based on a sample survey, such as the CPS, but on such general sources as employers' wage reports under Social Security, records of disbursement by government agencies to individuals, income-tax returns, and industrial and population censuses. OBE personal income series estimates are published annually in the April issue of *Survey of Current Business*. A description of the general background and methodology of the OBE estimates is given in U.S. Office of Business Economics, *U.S. Income and Output* (Washington, Government Printing Office, 1958).

The two agencies mentioned use different definitions of income. The OBE definition, but not that of the CPS, includes among other items the following types of nonmoney income: wages in kind, value of food and fuel produced and consumed on farms, and net rental value of owner-occupied house. On the other hand, the CPS definition, but not that of the OBE, includes income from boarders and roomers, regular contributions towards support made by persons not living in the household, and some other items. Evidence exists that those interviewed in the CPS tend to understate their incomes considerably. The net effect of these differences is that OBE figures average consider-

164

ably higher. When reading discussions about poverty it is well to be aware of the source of the statistics on income quoted by the author.

The Decennial Census, the CPS, and the OBE personal series are the principal, but not the only, federal sources of income data. They can be supplemented by the Old Age, Survivors, and Disability Insurance earnings record data, the Department of Agriculture farm income series, and the federal income-tax data. See U.S. Office of Statistical Standards, *Statistical Services of the United States Government* (rev. ed.; Washington, Government Printing Office, 1963) for a good general account.

An excellent nongovernmental source of income statistics is the annual Survey of Consumer Finances conducted by the Survey Research Center of the University of Michigan. Like the CPS, it is a sample survey, though conducted on a much smaller scale. The Survey is useful, in spite of its modest sample size, on account of the wide variety of questions asked in each interview. See George Katona and others, *1962 Survey of Consumer Finances* (Ann Arbor, University of Michigan Press, 1963).

In the discussion of poverty in Chapter 5 of this book, the term was defined by using the SSA Poverty Index which was developed by Mollie Orshansky of the Division of Research and Statistics, U.S. Social Security Administration. Probably the nearest thing to an official estimate of the extent of poverty in the country is that contained in *Annual Report of the Council of Economic Advisers,* accompanying the *Economic Report of the President, 1964* (Washington, Government Printing Office,

1964), pp. 57–59, and the 1965 *Report,* pp. 162–65. In both of these the Orshansky figures were cited, though without explicit mention of source.

As was remarked in the text, it is an interesting fact that a number of recent studies on the extent of poverty, although using approaches quite different from that of the SSA Poverty Index, nevertheless arrive at quite similar results. All of them place the proportion of poor in the country at something like one-fifth of the total population. The consensus is striking. It gives one confidence in the validity of the estimate.

The year 1960 is considered in *Poverty and Deprivation in the United States* (Washington, Conference on Economic Progress, 1962). Income figures were taken from the OBE personal income series. Poverty was defined as an annual income of less than $4,000 for families or less than $2,000 for unattached individuals. On this basis, the study concludes that about 34 million persons in families and about 4 million unattached individuals were poor; this is a little more than a fifth of the nation.

Lenore A. Epstein in "Unmet Need in a Land of Abundance" (*Social Security Bulletin,* May, 1963, pp. 3–11) chose "a very conservative definition of low income—the taxable limit for income under present Federal tax laws." Thus she defined as poor, families and individuals who did not have to pay income tax. Using this criterion and 1959 CPS income figures she concluded that about 33 million were poor. This is somewhat less than one-fifth of the population.

The Joint Economic Committee of the U.S. Congress commissioned Robert J. Lampman, an economist from the University of Michigan, to study what progress was being made in the conquest of poverty. His report, "The Low Income Population and Economic Growth," was published by the Committee in *Joint Committee Print,* 86th Congress, 1st Session, Study Papers Nos. 12 and 13 (Washington, Government Printing Office, 1959). Lampman speaks of "low income," rather than "poverty," but he seems to regard the terms as synonymous. He chose different cutoff points for families of different sizes, and used CPS income data. His conclusion was that about 19 per cent of the population was in the "low-income status" in 1957.

A study made at the Survey Research Center of the University of Michigan is reported and analyzed in James N. Morgan and Others, *Income and Welfare in the United States* (New York, McGraw-Hill, 1962). Data were gathered in an independent sample survey. Criteria of poverty included both liquid assets and current income. The year studied was 1959. The report concluded that "there are some 10.4 million poor families in the United States." Compare this with the estimate of the Council of Economic Advisers that there were 9.3 million poor families in 1962, and it will be clear that the Survey Research Center estimates are not out of line.

A number of other estimates, based on informed opinion, rather than on formal studies, give quite similar results. For example, the viewpoint of the AFL-CIO is expressed in *America's Haves and Have Nots* (reprint from *Labor's Economic Review,* August, 1960) as follows: "The conclusion is inescapable that today at least 20 per cent of all Americans—one-fifth of the nation—live close to the poverty line—or below it." Michael Harrington in his excellent book *The Other America* (New York, Macmillan, 1962), p. 182, states that "somewhere between 20 and 25 per cent of the American people are poor."

NOTES

[1] See the famous exchange of letters between the Emperor Trajan and Pliny the Younger, his legate to Bithynia, in Pliny's *Letters*, Book 10, nos. 96 and 97.

[2] For a good discussion of natural law, see J. Messner, *Social Ethics. Natural Law in the Modern World* (St. Louis, B. Herder, 1949).

[3] The term is due to William Graham Sumner. See his *Folkways* (Boston, Ginn, 1940; originally published, 1906).

[4] Quoted in S. E. Morison and H. S. Commager, *The Growth of the American Republic* (New York, Oxford University Press, 1930), p. 126.

[5] See Thomas Verner Moore, *Dynamic Psychology* (Philadelphia, Lippincott, 1924), for his concept of the parataxes. The book is still valuable. For a more modern treatment, see A. P. Noyes and L. C. Kolb, *Modern Clinical Psychiatry* (6th ed.; Philadelphia, Saunders, 1963), Chapter 4, "Mental Mechanisms and Their Functions."

[6] An example of such pseudo-science is Nathaniel Weyl, *The Negro in American Civilization* (Washington, Public Affairs Press, 1960). For the genuine scientific position, see "Science and the Race Problem: A Report of the AAAS Committee on Science in the Promotion of Human Welfare," in *Science*, 142 (1963), pp. 558–61.

[7] Mt. 23, 23. In scriptural citations here and throughout the book standard English versions have been freely used. However, they have always been compared with the original text and the present writer has not hesitated to use his own translations when this seemed desirable.

[8] The three virtues are, in the Greek text, *krisis, eleos,* and *pistis*. The ordinary meaning of *krisis* is "judgment," but here it is used in the sense of "right judgment," that is, "justice." *Pistis* is "faith," but in this context it does not refer to faith in divine revelation, but to "faithfulness" in carrying out the obligations one has assumed.

[9] Mt. 23, 24.

CHAPTER TWO

¹ On American slavery in general, two excellent references are Ulrich B. Phillips, *American Negro Slavery* (New York, Peter Smith, 1952, originally published, 1918) and Kenneth M. Stampp, *The Peculiar Institution* (New York, Knopf, 1956). For an excellent critical essay on slavery as a problem in historiography, see Stanley M. Elkins, *Slavery* (Chicago, University of Chicago Press, 1959), pp. 1–26. An excellent book on the Atlantic slave trade is Daniel P. Mannix, *Black Cargoes* (New York, Viking, 1962).

² The Constitution, Article I, Section 9, forbade legislation against the slave trade before this date.

³ More exactly, 697,681 and 3,953,760.

⁴ There was also some trade with East Africa. On this, see Mannix, *Black Cargoes,* Chapter 11.

⁵ *Ibid.,* p. 287.

⁶ See *ibid.,* Chapter 5, for details on the Middle Passage including the facts mentioned in the text.

⁷ Such pampering, says Stampp, "gave its recipient privileges and comforts but made him into something less than a man." *The Peculiar Institution,* p. 327.

⁸ William D. Postell, *Health of Slaves on Southern Plantations* (Baton Rouge, Louisiana State University Press, 1951).

⁹ The point is developed in Elkins, *Slavery,* and in Charles E. Silberman, *Crisis in Black and White* (New York, Random House, 1964).

¹⁰ On punishments, see Stampp, *The Peculiar Institution,* Chapter 4.

¹¹ Murder is still a tool for white supremacists in the Deep South. See William B. Huie, *Three Lives for Mississippi* (New York, WCC Books, 1965).

¹² Frederic Bancroft, *Slave-Trading in the Old South* (Baltimore, Furst, 1931), Chapter 9, gives abundant details.

¹³ Frederick Douglass, *Narrative of the Life of Frederick Douglass, an American Slave.* Edited by Benjamin Quarles (Cambridge, Harvard University Press, 1960; originally published, 1845), pp. 94–95.

¹⁴ Elkins, *Slavery,* pp. 63–80, gives a good summary of slavery in Latin American countries.

[15] The parallel between the concentration camps and American slavery is developed by Elkins, *ibid.,* pp. 103–15.

[16] Walter H. Mazyck, *George Washington and the Negro* (Washington, Associated Publishers, 1932), and Matthew T. Mellon, *Early American Views on Negro Slavery* (Boston, Meador, 1934).

[17] The Quakers opposed slavery. Baptists and Methodists split into northern and southern churches. A good study on the Methodists is Charles B. Swaney, *Episcopal Methodism and Slavery* (Boston, Badger, 1926).

[18] Madeleine Hooke Rice, *American Catholic Opinion in the Slavery Controversy* (New York, Columbia University Press, 1944), and John C. Murphy, *An Analysis of the Attitudes of American Catholics toward the Immigrant and the Negro, 1825–1925* (Washington, Catholic University Press, 1940).

[19] Rice, *American Catholic Opinion,* pp. 27, 33, and 46.

[20] *Ibid.,* p. 46.

[21] *Ibid.,* p. 141.

[22] Roger Baudier, *The Catholic Church in Louisiana* (New Orleans, Roger Baudier, 1939), pp. 121 and 145. Rice, *ibid.,* p. 47.

[23] Rice, *op. cit.,* p. 49.

[24] Baudier, *The Catholic Church in Louisiana,* pp. 108–9.

[25] *Ibid.,* p. 160.

[26] Rice, *op. cit.,* p. 139.

[27] *Ibid.,* pp. 118–23.

[28] See standard theologians, but particularly the article "Esclavage" by J. Dutilleul in *Dictionnaire de théologie catholique* (Paris, Letouzey, 1909–50), vol. 5, cols. 457–520.

[29] Mannix, *Black Cargoes,* p. 123.

[30] Fitzhugh's tract, along with two other tracts on the subject has been published with an Introduction by Harvey Wish under the title *Ante-Bellum* (New York, Capricorn Books, 1960).

[31] See the edition just mentioned, pp. 88–9.

[32] The classic work from our standpoint is Melville J. Herskovits, *The Myth of the Negro Past* (New York, Harper, 1941). There is a good critical summary in Elkins, *Slavery,* pp. 89–98.

[33] For a good review of recent literature, see R. M. Dreger and K. S.

Miller, "Comparative Psychological Studies of Negroes and Whites in the United States," in *Psychological Bulletin*, 57 (1960), pp. 361–402, supplemented by R. M. Dreger, "Comparative Psychological Studies of Negroes and Whites in the United States: A Reclarification," in *ibid.*, 60 (1963), pp. 35–39. See also the statement quoted in Chapter 1, note 6, above.

[34] An influential group of Americans believed that the solution of the slavery problem would be the eventual emancipation of the slaves who would then be returned to Africa. The American Colonization Society was the backbone of this movement, which resulted finally in the foundation of Liberia. See P. J. Staudenraus, *The African Colonization Movement, 1816–1865* (New York, Columbia University Press, 1961).

[35] Stampp, *The Peculiar Institution*, p. 108.

[36] *Ibid.*, p. 118.

[37] Phillips, *American Negro Slavery*, p. 488. See also Herbert Aptheker, *Negro Slave Revolts in the United States, 1526–1860* (New York, International Publishers, 1939).

CHAPTER THREE

[1] Raul Hilberg, *The Destruction of the European Jews* (Chicago, Quadrangle, 1961), p. 767, table. This is easily the best book on the subject, remarkably well documented. See also Gerald Reitlinger, *The Final Solution* (New York, Beechhurst Press, 1953) and Léon Poliakov, *Bréviaire de la haine* (Paris, Calmann-Lévy, 1951), translated as *Harvest of Hate* (Syracuse, Syracuse University Press, 1954).

[2] Georg von Rauch, *A History of Soviet Russia* (rev. ed.; New York, Praeger, 1957), p. 238.

[3] William L. Shirer, *The Rise and Fall of the Third Reich* (New York, Simon and Schuster, 1960), p. ix.

[4] A convenient edition is Anne Frank, *The Diary of a Young Girl*. Translated by B. M. Mooyaart-Doubleday (New York, Pocket Books, 1953).

[5] The difficulty exists also in this country. Wilbur B. Brookover and John B. Holland, "An Inquiry into the Meaning of Minority Group Attitude Expressions," in *American Sociological Review*, 17 (1952), pp. 196–202, report that members of the community they studied expressed "strongly unfavorable attitudes toward Jews." However, these people repeatedly misidentified as Jews persons who had no connection with Judaism. On

the other hand, many who actually were Jews were never identified as such.

⁶ Actually, the definition was a bit more complicated than is stated here. For a full discussion, see Hilberg, *Destruction,* pp. 43–53.

⁷ The German authorities officially distinguished three classes of camps: Type I, labor camps; Type II, somewhat more rigorous; and Type III, extermination camps. In the present chapter Types I and II are lumped together as "regular" or "ordinary" camps. The literature on concentration camps is rather extensive. Probably the most important single reference is Eugen Kogon, *Der SS-Staat,* translated as *The Theory and Practice of Hell* (New York, Farrar, Straus, and Cudahy, 1950). Two books by psychiatrists who were former camp inmates are valuable for the insight they give into camp psychology: Bruno Bettelheim, *The Informed Heart* (Glencoe, Free Press, 1960), and Viktor E. Frankl, *Man's Search for Meaning* (New York, Washington Square Press, 1963). There are many other descriptions of camp life by former inmates.

⁸ Kogon, *Theory and Practice,* pp. 249–50.

⁹ *Ibid.,* p. 251.

¹⁰ *Ibid.,* p. 249.

¹¹ *The Informed Heart,* pp. 145–46 and 160.

¹² Paul J. Guttmann, *Sexualtheorien und Konzentrationslager* (Berkeley, private edition, 1957), pp. 31–37, "Die Angriffe auf das Schamgefühl."

¹³ The so-called *Muselmänner* (Moslems). See Bettelheim, *Informed Heart,* pp. 151–53.

¹⁴ The account given here in the text is necessarily condensed and generalized. For details, see Hilberg, *Destruction,* pp. 177–256. Some use was made of gas vans during the mobile killing operations, but they were not considered very satisfactory. *Ibid.,* p. 219.

¹⁵ *Ibid.,* p. 767.

¹⁶ *Ibid.,* pp. 555–61.

¹⁷ For abundant detail, see *ibid.,* pp. 568–600.

¹⁸ *Ibid.,* p. 649.

¹⁹ Frankl, *Man's Search,* p. 134. Frankl tells of a camp commander who "paid no small sum of money from his own pocket in order to purchase medicines for his prisoners from the nearest market town" (*ibid.,* pp. 135–36).

[20] Hilberg, *Destruction*, p. 189.

[21] *Ibid.*, p. 649.

[22] William M. Harrigan, "Hochhuth as Historian," in *Continuum*, 2 (1964), pp. 166–82.

[23] Louis Tursky, "Could the Death Camps Have Been Bombed?" in *Jewish Frontier*, 31, no. 8 (1964), pp. 19–24.

[24] Although they do not deal specifically with the destruction of the Jews and although they consider the moral problems of the time only as they affected Catholics, the following are nevertheless illuminating discussions of the general confusion of conscience existing under Hitler: Gordon C. Zahn, *German Catholics and Hitler's Wars* (New York, Sheed and Ward, 1962); the same author's *In Solitary Witness* (New York, Holt, Rinehart and Winston, 1964); and Mother Mary Alice Gallin, *Ethical and Religious Factors in the German Resistance to Hitler* (Washington, Catholic University Press, 1955).

CHAPTER FOUR

[1] See the account by Father Alberto de Onaindía in Robert Payne (editor), *The Civil War in Spain* (New York, Premier Books, 1964), pp. 191–95. Hermann Kesten, *Die Kinder von Gernika* (Amsterdam, Allert de Lange, 1939), is a novel which presents the bombing as seen through children's eyes.

[2] *The City We Loved* (Coventry, Three Spires, 1942)

[3] There is a fairly detailed account of the development of policy in U.S. Air Force. U.S.A.F. Historical Division, *The Army Air Forces in World War II* (7 vols.; Chicago, University of Chicago Press, 1948–58), vol. 2, chapters 7–12.

[4] A good general treatment is Hans Rumpf, *The Bombing of Germany* (New York, Holt, Rinehart and Winston, 1963; original German edition, 1961). On Dresden, see also David Irving, *The Destruction of Dresden* (New York, Holt, Rinehart and Winston, 1964), and Axel Rodenberger, *Der Tod von Dresden* (Dortmund, Franz Müller-Rodenberger, 1952).

[5] *Army Air Forces*, vol. 5, pp. 615–17.

[6] These figures are given in U.S. Atomic Energy Commission, *The Effects of Nuclear Weapons* (rev. ed.; Washington, Government Printing Office, 1962), p. 550. Others have suggested higher figures.

[7] For an excellent summary of the effects of nuclear weapons on human beings, see the reference just cited, Chapter 11.

[8] Michihiko Hachiya, *Hiroshima Diary* (Chapel Hill, University of North Carolina Press, 1955), p. 14. See also John A. Siemes, S. J., "Hiroshima: Eye-Witness," *Saturday Review of Literature,* 29 (May 11, 1946), pp. 24–25 and 40–44.

[9] Rumpf, *Bombing of Germany,* p. 82, table 4.

[10] *Army Air Forces,* vol. 3, p. 802.

[11] U.S. Strategic Bombing Survey, *The Effects of Strategic Bombing on the German War Economy* (Washington, Overall Economic Effects Division, 1945), p. 39.

[12] Rumpf, *Bombing of Germany,* p. 204.

[13] See the letter, Truman to Cate, reproduced between pp. 712 and 713, *Army Air Forces,* vol. 5.

[14] *Ibid.,* p. 726.

[15] *Ibid.,* p. 710. The whole of Chapter 23 is useful for background information.

[16] For an account of the Alamogordo test, see Henry DeW. Smyth, *Atomic Energy for Military Purposes* (Princeton, Princeton University Press, 1945), Appendix 6. The book is a very useful introduction to the physics of nuclear energy and to the history of the atom bomb.

[17] John C. Ford, "The Morality of Obliteration Bombing," in *Theological Studies,* 5 (1944), pp. 261–309. Quotation on p. 273.

[18] "The immunity of non-combatants from direct attack is one of the fundamental rules of the International Law of war." L. Oppenheim, *International Law,* 2 vols. (6th ed.; New York, Longmans, 1940), vol. 2, p. 413. Note that this book was published during the Second World War and is therefore a good witness for contemporary thought.

[19] Oppenheim, *ibid.,* p. 203, states that under the laws of war even some members of the armed forces cannot be considered combatants. He lists as examples "couriers, doctors, farriers, veterinary surgeons, chaplains, nurses, official and voluntary ambulance men, contractors, canteen-caterers, newspaper correspondents, civil servants, diplomatists, and foreign military attachés." If these are to be given noncombatant status and considered immune from direct attack, it would seem logical that munitions workers should share the same immunity. However, for the sake of argument, we are accepting the more difficult alternative.

174

20 See Ford, "Morality of Obliteration Bombing," pp. 283–84, for a long list of examples.

21 Ford, *ibid.*, pp. 284–88.

22 Since the end of the Second World War there has been a good deal of discussion among moral theologians and publicists as to whether *any* conceivable cause could justify a war in which nuclear energy would be used as a weapon. The question is of the most critical importance but it will not be discussed here because it lies outside the scope of the chapter.

23 *AAS*, 32 (1940), pp. 146–50.

24 *AAS*, 35 (1943), pp. 9–24.

25 The silence of Catholics on obliteration bombing was not the only example of their failure to evaluate national war policies in the light of moral principles. In fact, as Father John Courtney Murray has well said, "The classic example . . . was the policy of 'unconditional surrender' during the last war. This policy clearly violated the requirement of the 'right intention' that has always been a principle in the traditional doctrine of war. Yet no sustained criticism was made of the policy by Catholic spokesmen." "Remarks on the Moral Problem of War," in *Theological Studies,* 20 (1959), pp. 40–61. Quotation on p. 54.

26 On the fate of German conscientious objectors, see Zahn, *German Catholics and Hitler's Wars.* See also the same author's article, "The Case for Christian Dissent," in *Breakthrough to Peace* (Norfolk, New Directions, 1962), pp. 117–38.

27 Paul Hanly Furfey, "Bombing of Noncombatants Is Murder," in *The Catholic C.O.,* 2 (July-September, 1945), pp. 3–4. This was before Hiroshima.

28 In a wartime study 248 college students were presented with the proposition, "The real American should be willing to fight for his country whether it is in the right or the wrong." More than half either approved or were undecided. H. S. Conrad and R. N. Sanford, "Some Specific War-Attitudes of College Students," in *Journal of Psychology,* 17 (1944), pp. 153–86.

29 In his 1956 Christmas Broadcast (*AAS*, 49 [1957], pp. 5–22), Pope Pius XII made a statement which some interpreted as a repudiation of conscientious objection. It is important enough to deserve full quotation.

"Under present circumstances it is clearly possible that a situation could arise in a nation such that, every effort to maintain peace having been exhausted, a defensive war offering a good hope of success against unjust attacks could not be considered unlawful.

"If, therefore, an assembly representative of the people and a government, both chosen in free elections, in a moment of extreme necessity and using legitimate measures of internal and external policy, set up measures of defense taking whatever plans they consider necessary, they do not act immorally. Therefore a Catholic citizen could not appeal to his own conscience to refuse to serve and to carry out the duties imposed by the laws."

It should be quite obvious that this declaration does not state that conscientious objection is illegitimate in general. It states merely that it would be illegitimate in an extreme, but possible situation. For a very well-balanced discussion of the passage and of the teaching on conscientious objection in general, see René Coste, *Le Problème du droit de guerre dans la pensée de Pie XII* (Paris, Aubier, 1962), pp. 365–77, and the same author's *Morale internationale* (Tournai, Desclée, 1964), pp. 445–64.

[30] Discourse of Pope Paul VI, Castel Gandolfo, Italy, August 8, 1965. The Second Vatican Council was quite explicit in condemning the bombing of civilians. "Any act of war aimed indiscriminately at the destruction of entire cities or of extensive areas along with their population is a crime against God and man himself. It merits unequivocal and unhesitating condemnation." *Constitution on the Church in the Modern World,* Paragraph 80.

[31] "At times it is the positive duty of a nation to wage war in the defense of life and right. Our country now finds itself in such circumstances." *The Bishops' Statement on Victory and Peace,* November 14, 1942.

CHAPTER FIVE

[1] See Paul Hanly Furfey, "Christ as *Tektôn*," in *Catholic Biblical Quarterly,* 17 (1955), pp. 324–35, for a discussion of the nature of Christ's work and the status of skilled workers in first-century Palestine.

[2] Robert L. Heilbroner, *The Great Ascent* (New York, Harper and Row, 1963), is a good introductory discussion of poverty in the undeveloped countries and its remedies.

[3] Helen H. Lamale and Margaret S. Stotz, "The Interim City Worker's

Family Budget," Reprint no. 2346 from the *Monthly Labor Review* (August, 1960). See also Margaret S. Stotz, "The BLS Interim Budget for a Retired Couple," Reprint no. 2354 from the *Monthly Labor Review* (November, 1960).

[4] On sources of information about incomes, see the Appendix. An excellent source of current economic information is the monthly *Economic Indicators,* prepared for the Joint Economic Committee by the Council of Economic Advisers and available from the Government Printing Office at $2.50 a year.

[5] Mollie Orshansky, "Who's Who Among the Poor: A Demographic View of Poverty," in *Social Security Bulletin,* 28 (July 1965), pp. 3–32. For background see the same author's articles, "Counting the Poor," in *ibid.* (January, 1965), pp. 3–29 and "Children of the Poor," in *ibid.* (July, 1963), pp. 3–13.

[6] For details, see the Appendix.

[7] If the poor are defined as those living in families with incomes below $3,000, plus unrelated individuals with incomes under $1,500, results are quite similar to those obtained with the SSA test. See Orshansky, "Counting the Poor," Table 1, Columns A and D. In 1964 about 9.5 per cent of American families had incomes under $2,000 and 26.0 per cent of unrelated individuals had incomes under $1,000. Thus these families and unrelated individuals had incomes less than two-thirds of the cut-off minimums. *Current Population Reports, Consumer Income,* Series P-60, no. 44 (May 27, 1965), p. 2.

[8] The proportion fluctuates from month to month. For 1965 as a whole, an average of 19.6 per cent of those at work in nonagricultural industries worked less than 35 hours a week.

[9] *Manpower Report of the President and a Report on Manpower Requirements, Resources, Utilization, and Training by the United States Department of Labor* (Washington, Government Printing Office, 1965) discusses the underutilization of manpower on pp. 30–31.

[10] George N. Putnam and Edna M. O'Hern, *The Status Significance of an Isolated Urban Dialect,* Supplement to *Language,* vol. 31, no. 4, part 2 (October-December, 1955).

[11] It does not take an expert to recognize subproletarian speech for what it is. This fact was demonstrated during the study just mentioned by the

177

following experiment: Specimens of the speech of twelve persons were recorded on tape. The recording in each case was a short fable which was read to the subject and which he was then asked to repeat in his own words. Three of the subjects were alley dwellers. The other nine were chosen to represent a wide range of social status. There were three university professors, a bookkeeper, a stenographer, two skilled workmen, and two maids. The recordings were arranged in random order and played to a group of teachers and graduate students who were then asked to express on a rating scale their judgments of the social status of the various speakers. The results were quite remarkable. Although the recordings were very short, averaging 100 to 150 words in length, and although there were absolutely no other clues as to the speakers' identity, those who heard the recordings were able to judge the social status of the speakers with remarkable accuracy. By speaking only a few sentences a subproletarian betrays his social status. See *ibid.*, pp. 25–28.

[12] Some of the peculiarities of the alley dialect have been found also in various local dialects in the eastern part of the country. See Putnam and O'Hern, *ibid.*, pp. 23–24, notes 17 and 18; E. Bagby Atwood, *A Survey of Verb Forms in the Eastern United States* (Ann Arbor, University of Michigan Press, 1953); and Hans Kurath, *A Word Geography of the Eastern United States* (Ann Arbor, University of Michigan Press, 1949).

[13] *Current Population Reports, Consumer Income,* Series P-60, no. 43 (September 29, 1964), p. 25; and *ibid.*, no. 45 (June 18, 1965), p. 3. See also Denis F. Johnston, "Educational Attainment of Workers, March 1964," in *Monthly Labor Review,* 88 (1965), pp. 517–27.

[14] Frank Riessman, *The Culturally Deprived Child* (New York, Harper, 1962), Chapter 6, "The Hidden I.Q."

[15] *Ibid.,* Chapter 2, "Are the Culturally Deprived Interested in Education?"

[16] An unpublished report by Harlem Youth Opportunities Unlimited (commonly known by the acronym HARYOU) entitled *Youth in the Ghetto* (New York, Harlem Youth Opportunities Unlimited, 1964) has an excellent discussion of the causes of underachievement by slum children in Chapter 6, "Education in Central Harlem." The Bureau of Social Research of the Catholic University of America is at present engaged in a research project called "The Intellectual Stimulation of Culturally De-

prived Infants" which is financed by a grant from the National Institute of Mental Health. An experimental group of about thirty fifteen-month-old infants and a control group of equal size are being chosen from families of poor and poorly educated parents. All infants are tested at the beginning on the Bayley Infant Scale of Mental Development and will be retested at intervals over a period of about two years. Tutors visit the infants in the experimental group for an hour a day, five days a week. By toys, pictures, speech, and visits to interesting places, the tutors endeavor to stimulate the child, arouse his interest in his environment, teach manipulative skills, and develop language. At this writing it is still too early to talk about results. However, the present writer, who is acting as project director, was very much impressed by the fact that the average I.Q.s of the children in the experimental and control groups together was slightly over 106. Thus there is no evidence of mental inferiority among slum children at this age. It will be interesting to see whether the children in the experimental group, under the stimulus of tutoring, will retain their good intelligence better than the children in the control group who will be without this stimulation.

[17] August B. Hollingshead, *Elmtown's Youth* (New York, Wiley, 1949), especially pp. 180–85.

[18] James B. Conant, "Social Dynamite in Our Large Cities," in *Social Dynamite,* the report of the Conference on Unemployed, Out-of-School Youth in Urban Areas, May 24–26, 1961 (Washington, National Committee for Children and Youth, 1961), pp. 26–42. See particularly p. 34.

[19] Riessman, *The Culturally Deprived Child,* Chapter 3, "Discrimination Without Prejudice." See also James H. S. Bossard, *The Sociology of Child Development* (rev. ed.; New York, Harper, 1954), pp. 337–40.

[20] Jacob Landers, "The Higher Horizons Program in New York City," in *Programs for the Educationally Disadvantaged,* Report of a Conference on Teaching Children Who Are Educationally Disadvantaged, May 21–23, 1962 (Washington, Government Printing Office, 1963), pp. 45–56. Quotation on p. 48.

[21] Robert L. Stein, "Work History, Attitudes, and Income of the Unemployed," in *Monthly Labor Review,* 86 (1963), pp. 1405–13. See pp. 1410–11. Of course, many in the subproletariat are not "unemployed" in the technical sense, but are "not in the labor force." That is to say, for one

reason or another, such as age, disability, or a very low work aptitude, they are not actively seeking employment.

22 *Ibid.*, p. 1405.

23 U.S. National Center for Health Statistics, *Medical Care, Health Status, and Family Income, United States* (Vital and Health Statistics, Series 10, no. 9; Washington, Government Printing Office, 1964), p. 71.

24 *Ibid.*, p. 55. There were, indeed, wide differences of disability among various age groups; but the same wide class differences appeared in all of them.

25 U.S. Public Health Service. National Vital Statistics Division, *Mortality by Occupation and Industry* (Vital Statistics, Special Reports, vol. 53, no. 2; Washington, Government Printing Office, 1962), p. 57. This report contains a valuable review of previous studies in the area.

26 *Ibid.*, Table 2, pp. 82–84.

27 There are a few rather rare diseases genetically confined to particular ethnic groups. Thus sickle-cell anemia seems to be confined to Negroes. However, these facts are not important enough to disturb the generalization of the text.

28 U.S. Bureau of the Census, *Statistical Abstract of the United States: 1964* (Washington, Government Printing Office, 1964), p. 57.

29 *Ibid.*, p. 55. See also Helen C. Chase, "White-Nonwhite Mortality Differentials in the United States," in *Health, Education, and Welfare Indicators* (June, 1965), pp. 27–37.

30 U.S. National Center for Health Statistics, *Medical Care, Health Status, Family Income,* pp. 24 and 6.

31 Alvin L. Schorr, *Slums and Social Insecurity* (Washington, Government Printing Office, 1963), p. 14.

32 Marion Ratigan, *A Sociological Survey of Disease in Four Alleys in the National Capital* (Washington, Catholic University of America Press, 1946), pp. 106–7.

33 In an effort to bridge the socio-cultural gap that isolates the slums, Dr. Gladys Sellew of the Department of Sociology of the Catholic University of America bought in February, 1936, a house in a segregated Negro Washington neighborhood and moved in with a group of women graduate students, white and colored. She named the residence Il Poverello House. Two years later her colleague Dr. Mary Elizabeth Walsh joined

the group, but left in 1940 to found another informal settlement house which was named Fides House. Both Il Poverello House and the original Fides House were adjacent to inhabited alleys, a notorious feature of Washington life in those days. Of course, the foundation of these settlements was not without precedent. The general settlement-house movement has a history stretching back to the 1880's. More directly, the Washington houses were influenced by Dorothy Day and her Catholic Worker houses in New York and elsewhere, and later by the Baroness de Hueck and her Friendship Houses. These, in turn, might be considered aspects of a broader Catholic social and intellectual trend of the period which included Dom Virgil Michel's liturgical movement and Graham Carey's Catholic art revival. What the two Washington houses contributed was a certain sociological sophistication. The residents made a number of formal studies; in addition, they tried to understand and explain the slum culture by participant observation, by living in close contact with slum life. Most of the statements made in the paragraphs that follow are based on experience gained at Il Poverello House and Fides House in the 1930's and 1940's. Fides House is now a large neighborhood center managed by the Missionary Servants of the Most Holy Trinity.

[34] Paul Mundy, *The Negro Boy Worker in Washington, D.C.* (Abstract of a Ph.D. dissertation; Washington, Catholic University Press, 1951), reported that, in a sample of Negro boys applying for work permits in Washington, about seven-eighths had jobs in one of six occupations, namely, messenger, porter, helper, bus boy, dishwasher, stock boy. On the high unemployment rates of teen-agers, particularly nonwhite males, see *Manpower Report of the President 1965,* pp. 26–29 and 206.

[35] Mary Elizabeth Walsh, "The Families of Marginally Employed Negro Workers in Washington, D.C.," in Paul H. Furfey, Thomas J. Harte, and Mary Elizabeth Walsh, *Marginal Employability* (Studies from the Bureau of Social Research, no. 2; Washington, Catholic University Press, 1962), pp. 29–43. See also Mary Elizabeth Walsh, "Cultural Disorganization of the Negro Family in an Area of Economic Blight," in *American Catholic Sociological Review,* 7 (1946), pp. 96–106; and her "Profiles of the Negro Family in an Area of Economic Blight," in *ibid.,* pp. 154–62. Even in religious matters the slum dweller meets discrimination. This fact was brought home vividly by the following incident. At

Il Poverello House some seminarians had interested a group of neighbor-hood people in the Church and at a certain point the group wished to begin attending Sunday Mass. However, they were embarrassed and dismayed at the prospect of attending the local Catholic church. It was not a question of race. Both they and the church's congregation were colored. It was a question of social class. Lower-class Negroes simply felt so awkward in the presence of middle-class Negroes that they were upset at the prospect of worshiping together. As a result, a special Mass had to be arranged for them in a vacant hall.

[36] Juvenile Delinquency Evaluation Project, *Delinquency in the Great City* (Final Report no. II; New York, Juvenile Delinquency Evaluation Project, 1961), p. 25. The present writer served as Assistant Director of the Project.

[37] Sophia M. Robison, *A Study of the Youthful Delinquent Behavior of Men Who Are Respectable Members of Society* (Garden City, Adelphi University Press, 1965). This work includes a valuable review of earlier research on the topic.

[38] Edwin H. Sutherland and Donald R. Cressey, *Principles of Criminology* (5th ed.; Philadelphia, Lippincott, 1955), particularly pp. 38–47.

[39] A number of books have been published recently on this topic. Besides those listed in the Appendix, the following should be noted: Ben H. Bagdikian, *In the Midst of Plenty: The Poor in America* (Boston, Beacon Press, 1964); Gabriel Kolko, *Wealth and Power in America* (New York, Praeger, 1962); and Gunnar Myrdal, *Challenge to Affluence* (New York, Pantheon Books, 1963).

[40] Hollingshead, *Elmtown's Youth,* pp. 110–11. Celia Burns Stendler, *Children of Brasstown* (Urbana, University of Illinois, 1949), gives an interesting analysis of the growth of class attitudes in schoolchildren.

[41] Gerald Kahn and Ellen J. Perkins, "Families Receiving AFDC: What Do They Have to Live on?," in *Welfare in Review,* 2 (October, 1964), pp. 7–15. Quotation on p. 7. The given figure does not include vendor pay-ments for medical care. There is evidence that the situation has not changed greatly since 1961.

[42] U.S. Welfare Administration, *Monthly Cost Standards for Basic Needs Used by States for Specified Types of Old-Age Assistance Cases and Families Receiving Aid to Families with Dependent Children, Jan-*

uary 1963 (Release reproduced from typewritten copy). The family discussed is, more concretely, one consisting of a mother (35), boy (14), girl (9), and girl (4), living in rented quarters.

[43] The option was available not only in the fifty states, but also in the District of Columbia, Puerto Rico, the Virgin Islands, and Guam.

[44] Mary R. Baker, "Personnel in Social Work," in *Encyclopedia of Social Work* (New York, National Association of Social Workers, 1965), pp. 532–40.

[45] Edgar May, *The Wasted Americans* (New York, Harper and Row, 1964), was written by a newspaper reporter who temporarily took a job as a welfare worker and wrote up his experiences.

[46] Mt. 25, 45.

CHAPTER SIX

[1] Kenneth M. Stampp, *The Peculiar Institution* (New York, Knopf, 1956), p. 211.

[2] Zahn, *German Catholics and Hitler's Wars,* p. 54.

[3] "L'Etat, considéré d'une manière générale comme société, c'est-à-dire la société civile, peut se définir: 'Une société humaine, juridique et universelle, qui a pour but de conduire ses membres à leur plus grande perfection dans l'ordre matériel et temporel.'" E. Valton, "Etat," in *Dictionnaire de théologie catholique,* 15 vols. (Paris, Letouzey, 1909–50), vol. 5, cols. 879–905.

[4] Mother Mary Alice Gallin, *Ethical and Religious Factors in the German Resistance to Hitler,* contains illuminating material.

[5] Mt. 23, 23.

[6] Maurice Bardèche in his book *Nuremberg ou la Terre Promise* makes the point that the trials were intended less to prove the guilt of the vanquished than the innocence of the victors. We have seen this book only in its Italian translation, *I servi della democratia* (Milan, Longanesi, 1949).

[7] *Trials of War Criminals Before the Nuernberg Military Tribunals* (Washington, Govrnment Printing Office, 1949–), vol. 4, p. 357.

[8] "The subordinate is bound only to obey the lawful orders of his superior and if he accepts a criminal order and executes it with a malice

of his own, he may not plead superior orders in mitigation of his offense."
Trials of War Criminals, vol. 4, pp. 470–71.

[9] U.S. Air Force. U.S.A.F. Historical Division, *The Army Air Forces in World War II,* 7 vols. (Chicago, University of Chicago Press, 1948–58), vol. 5, p. 716.

[10] *Ibid.,* p. 717.

[11] The New York *Herald Tribune* of August 7, 1965, carried an account of a reunion held in New York by the veterans of the 393d Bombardment Squadron on the twentieth anniversary of Hiroshima. There they enjoyed themselves, gave interviews, posed for pictures, and mingled freely with other citizens. There was no hint in the newspaper account that these veterans felt the least guilt or shame.

CHAPTER SEVEN

[1] The lawyer was quoting Dt. 6, 5, and Lev. 19, 18.

[2] Mt. 5, 17.

[3] Mt. 19, 21.

[4] Sir. 50, 25–26.

[5] Jn. 4, 9.

[6] 4 Kgs. 18, 11, and 17, 24. See the excellent discussion in Giuseppe Ricciotti, *The History of Israel,* 2 vols. (Milwaukee, Bruce, 1955), vol. 2, pp. 147–54.

[7] It is not to be inferred that the just actually did not understand the connection between love of neighbor and love of God; for this truth is basic. Perhaps the question reflects their astonishment at the disproportion between the overwhelming reward and the quality of their own good works which they evaluate with humility. In any case, the question put in their mouths serves to dramatize the point which Christ is making.

[8] Rom. 13, 8.

[9] Mary Elizabeth Walsh, *The Saints and Social Work* (Silver Spring, Maryland, Preservation of the Faith, 1937), is a study of a group of recent saints and beati in their relations to the poor. The importance of the works of mercy in the lives of these holy people is brought out very clearly.

[10] Failure to practice Christian charity is more than an individual fault. There exists an organized opposition to the Christian ideal of a society

governed by charity. This is "the world" in the New Testament sense. See Paul Hanly Furfey, *Fire on the Earth* (New York, Macmillan, 1936), and *The Mystery of Iniquity* (Milwaukee, Bruce, 1944).

[11] Mk. 10, 23. The other quotations in this paragraph are from the verses following.

[12] Paul Hanly Furfey, "*Plousios* and Cognates in the New Testament," in *Catholic Biblical Quarterly,* 5 (1943), pp. 243–63.

[13] Lk. 13, 32.

[14] F. W. Farrar, *The Gospel According to St. Luke* (Cambridge, Cambridge University Press, 1884; reprinted, 1921), p. 291.

[15] Lk. 23, 6–12.

[16] There were apparently two incidents of this sort. St. John (2, 13–22) clearly associates one with the first Passover of the public ministry of Christ. The Synoptics (Mt. 21, 12–13; Mk. 11, 15–18; Lk. 19, 45) record a similar event associated with the last Passover just before the Passion. Some commentators hold that the descriptions in all four Gospels refer to a single event.

[17] Jn. 2, 15.

[18] Mk. 11, 18.

[19] Lk. 23, 2.

[20] Lk. 23, 5.

[21] Jn. 8, 3–11.

[22] Mt. 5, 39; Lk. 6, 29; and Mt. 10, 34.

[23] 1 Pet. 2, 21.

CHAPTER EIGHT

[1] Federal Bureau of Investigation, *Uniform Crime Reports: 1964* (Washington, Government Printing Office, 1965), pp. 6 and 16. The area reporting to the FBI accounts for 92 per cent of the national population. The figures exclude the justifiable killing of a felon by a police officer or a private citizen.

[2] Daniel P. Mannix, *Black Cargoes* (New York, Viking, 1962), p. 287.

[3] Issues of October, 1964; February, 1965; January, 1965; and December, 1961.

[4] 1 Tim. 6, 10.

[5] See especially his *Das Gesetz Christi,* 3 vols. (7th ed.; Freiburg, Wewel, 1963).

[6] New York, Macmillan, 1965.

[7] The projects were set up with funds made available by the U.S. Office of Manpower, Automation, and Training under the provisions of the Manpower Development and Training Act of 1962. The Act provided that the effectiveness of the projects should be studied by a neutral agency. Our Bureau was given contracts to make half a dozen such studies.

[8] Elbridge Sibley, *The Education of Sociologists in the United States* (New York, Russell Sage Foundation, 1963).

[9] Only 25 per cent of the sociology candidates made a score as *high* as 580; only 25 per cent of the physics candidates scored as *low* as 660. *Ibid.,* p. 81. Candidates from "education" did considerably worse. Sociologists did slightly better on verbal aptitude, a not surprising fact. *Ibid.,* p. 80.

[10] On the requirements for a valid sociological theory, see Paul Hanly Furfey, *The Scope and Method of Sociology* (New York, Harper, 1953; reissue with a new Introduction, New York, Cooper Square Publishers, 1965), Chapter 20.

[11] Pitirim A. Sorokin, *Fads and Foibles in Modern Sociology and Related Sciences* (Chicago, Regnery, 1956), Chapter 2. Evidently, a good many of Sorokin's fellow sociologists agreed with his incisive criticisms; for he was elected President of the American Sociological Society and served last year.

[12] All the examples are actual; but it seems unkind to give citations because these particular studies are no worse than many others.

[13] Some of the evidence is summarized in Furfey, *Scope and Method,* pp. 456–61.

[14] Max Weber probably did more than anyone else to establish this tradition. However, his concept of a "value-free" science and his reasons for advocating it have often been misunderstood. See Alvin W. Gouldner, "Anti-Minotaur, the Myth of a Value-Free Sociology," in *Social Problems,* 9 (1962), pp. 199–213.

[15] On the general problem of values in sociology, see the following publications of the present writer: *Scope and Method,* pp. 43–51 and 217–

25; "Value-Judgments in Sociology," in *American Catholic Sociological Review*, 7 (1946), pp. 83–95; and "Sociological Science and the Problem of Values," in Llewellyn Gross (editor), *Symposium on Sociological Theory* (Evanston, Row, Peterson, 1959) pp. 509–30.

[16] Some developments within the science of sociology seem equally promising. There has been a tendency recently for government agencies to call in sociologists as consultants, as research directors, or as administrators. The expectation is that sociologists have a special expertise which will be useful in practical situations. Sociology itself is developing in a way to meet these expectations. There is a new respect for applied sociology. Some of the new developments are reviewed in Marvin A. Sussman's Presidential Address before the Society for the Study of Social Problems, "The Social Problems of the Sociologist," in *Social Problems,* 11 (1964), pp. 215–25.

An increasing amount of financial assistance is being granted sociologists for research. Research carried out in the United States and reported in articles in the *American Sociological Review* during 1944 was supported by grants of one sort or another in only 6 per cent of the instances. In 1954 the proportion was 40 per cent; and in 1964 it was 73 per cent. The chief grantor has been the federal government. Estimated obligations for research and development in sociology by the federal government for 1965 amount to 21 million dollars (verified through a personal communication from the National Science Foundation). Although this amount is small compared to the amounts allotted to the physical, medical, and engineering sciences, it is nevertheless encouraging because it establishes a principle. What is happening in sociology and economics is also happening in other social sciences. A new generation of scientists is coming to grips with the realities of current society and there is every reason to believe that graduate education will adapt itself to the trend.

[17] For a summary of the neo-positivist position with references to the literature, see Furfey, *Scope and Method,* pp. 38–43.

INDEX

189

191